THE FIRST TIME
INVESTOR'S WORKBOOK

THE FIRST TIME INVESTOR'S WORKBOOK

A Hands-On Guide to Implementing a Successful Investment Plan

Joe John Duran, CFA
with
Larry Chambers

McGraw-Hill
New York   Chicago   San Francisco
Lisbon   London   Madrid   Mexico City
Milan   New Delhi   San Juan   Seoul
Singapore   Sydney   Toronto

Library of Congress Cataloging-in-Publication Data

Duran, Joe.
    The first time investor's workbook : a hands-on guide to implementing a successful investment plan / by Joe Duran and Larry Chambers.
      p. cm.
    ISBN 0-07-137054-4
    1. Investments. 2. Finance, Personal. I. Duran, Joe (Joseph J.) II. Chambers, Larry.
First time investor's. III. Title.

HG4521. C4515 2001
332.6—dc21   2001018297

McGraw-Hill

A Division of The McGraw·Hill Companies

1 2 3 4 5 6 7 8 9 0 CUS/CUS 0 9 8 7 6 5 4 3 2 1

ISBN 0-07-137054-4

This book was set in Times by Inkwell Publishing Services.

Printed and bound by Custom Printing.

This publication is designed to provide accurate and authoritative information in regard to the subject matter covered. It is sold with the understanding that neither the author nor the publisher is engaged in rendering legal, accounting, futures/securities trading, or other professional service. If legal advice or other expert assistance is required, the services of a competent professional person should be sought.

> *—From a Declaration of Principles jointly adopted by a Committee of the American Bar Association and a Committee of Publishers*

McGraw-Hill books are available at special quantity discounts to use as premiums and sales promotions, or for use in corporate training sessions. For more information, please write to the Director of Special Sales, Professional Publishing, McGraw-Hill, Two Penn Plaza, New York, NY 10121-2298. Or contact your local bookstore.

 This book is printed on recycled, acid-free paper containing a minimum of 50% recycled, de-inked fiber.

CONTENTS

Foreword   vii
Acknowledgments   ix

INTRODUCTION   1

What Will This Workbook Accomplish for You?   1
How to Use This Workbook   2
How This Workbook Is Organized   3
Special Features of This Workbook   4

SECTION ONE—GETTING STARTED   5

The Investment Policy Statement (IPS)   7
The Financial Success Diet   10
Mental Accounting   11
What Lifestyle Stage Are You In?   12
How Much Money Will You Need?   17
What Kind of Investor Are You?   19
The Five Personalities   20
The Lifeboat Drill   24
Recognizing Your Constraints   30
What Is Your Time Horizon?   30
Liquidity   31
Tax Rates   32
Legal Considerations   34
Unique Circumstances   35
Recap   36

SECTION TWO—THE RULES OF THE GAME   37

The Rules   37
The Six Concepts   41

Concept One: The Importance of Asset Allocation   42
Concept Two: Understanding Diversification   44
Concept Three: Combining Dissimilar Investments   46
Concept Four: Adding Time to Your Investment Program   47
Concept Five: The Magic of Compounding   50
Concept Six: Understanding Asset-Class Investing   52
How to Invest in These Asset Classes   57
Understanding the Vehicles—Mutual Funds   58
Understanding Your Instruction Manual—The Prospectus   63
Other Things You Should Know about Mutual Funds   65
How Do the Various Mutual Fund Parties Work Together?   68
Major Types of Mutual Funds   69
How to Read Newspaper Mutual Fund Tables   75
What If You've Bought a Bad Fund?   76
Exchange Traded Funds   77
Individually Managed Accounts   80
Investing Directly in Stocks   82
Understanding Fixed Income Securities   85
Investing Directly in Bonds   86
Investment Vehicles That Are Sheltered from Tax   90
Retirement Plan Vehicles   98
Concepts That Are Least Effective   100

SECTION THREE—APPLYING A DISCIPLINED STRATEGY   105

Completing Your Investment Policy Statement   105
What's a Reasonable Growth Rate of Return?   106
The Impact of Taxes   108
What Investments Are Appropriate?   110
Should You Do It Yourself or Work with an Advisor?   117
Questions to Ask an Advisor   119
Selecting a Financial Advisor   120
How Do Advisors Get Paid?   124
Doing It Yourself   126
Conclusion   132

Glossary   133
Index   151

FOREWORD

Over the course of my 35-year career in the financial services industry, I have witnessed the coming and going of many different investment trends. Often accompanied with promises of how they will make you more money or take away all the risk, these trends are always accompanied with the promise that *it'll be different this time.*

No one has found a risk-free way to make more money—nor will they. There are eternal truths to investing that will never change and the most important one is that the better prepared you are as an investor, the better you will fare.

Every investor has a constant tug-of-war between two key emotions: fear and greed. Both are very destructive to an investor. Being prepared—by that I mean being educated and having a plan—is the only way I know to help keep these dueling emotions at bay.

In this book you have a very sophisticated tool, one that will help you to be a better investor no matter what type of person you are. Joe has taken some of the complex investment methodologies used by financial professionals and academics and created a practical, easy-to-follow guide for all investors seeking to increase control of their financial futures.

The simplicity with which it reads belies the fact that it is giving you the most important truths to investing.

The end result is that, if you follow the steps outlined in this book, you will be preparing yourself for success—setting a course, mapping it out, and preparing for the road ahead. I know of no other way to succeed.

Robert W. Doede, Ph.D.
Chairman of the Board
Centurion Capital Group, Inc.

ACKNOWLEDGMENTS

Thanks to Jennifer, and to my whole family for their support, and to all the friends and acquaintances who have shared their insights and wisdom with me.

Also, a special note of thanks to Larry for all of his assistance in putting this book together, and to the research team at CCM for assembling so much of the data.

Joe John Duran

INTRODUCTION

Welcome to a workbook that may change the way you invest forever. Have you been suffering from that vague, indefinable feeling of doom that awakens many investors in the middle of the night? Do you feel your stress level go up every time you *think* about investing? Well *The First Time Investor's Workbook* was written for you.

WHAT WILL THIS WORKBOOK ACCOMPLISH FOR YOU?

The promise of this workbook is one of understanding and controlling your financial destiny. Why is this so important? Because, if you don't, there's a possibility that someone else will. There are always people who will take advantage of your lack of knowledge.

If you follow the strategies laid out in this workbook, you will have the peace of mind that comes from understanding the tactics you're using. Therefore, you will stay on the right path, which will ensure that your money is working as hard as you are. When you are confident with your information, you can then invest your *serious* money.

By serious money, we mean your *life-altering wealth*—that is, the money you earned and saved all your life and that you plan to live on throughout your retirement. Serious money has two goals: participation and protection. In other words, *grow it* and *make sure it doesn't disappear*.

Specifically, you will learn how to meet and overcome the four most important challenges that every first time investor must address in order to be successful:

1. Understanding your investment temperament
2. Designing a successful portfolio that works for you
3. Keeping life manageable
4. Staying the course

By the time you finish this workbook, the financial portion of your life will be well orchestrated, coordinated, and planned so you know what it is doing and why it is doing what it is doing. You won't look at the newspaper in fear of *how your money is doing*. You will know where you are headed, whether you should sit through declines, if you'll have enough money for retirement, and if you need to save more money. There is not a randomness to this path. You're not just *hoping* to survive—you're actually becoming knowledgeable and understanding what you're doing; thus, *ensuring* that you will survive.

HOW TO USE THIS WORKBOOK

In this workbook, we focus on the fundamental truths of investing. Control begins with first understanding yourself, then knowing the rules of the game, and finally, applying a disciplined strategy. Follow these three steps thoroughly and in sequence. Take your time, and remember you're starting a lifelong journey. This is the first step to a more successful investing future. This workbook is presented in a logical, proven, and systematic process (Exhibit I-1). If you take your time to do each step properly, you will have a structured investment policy statement that you can then either implement on your own, or work with an advisor to implement. Either way, you will have more knowledge, understanding, and a higher comfort level with the way your money is working for you.

We are going to introduce a *tool* that can help you answer all four investment challenges. It's called an investment policy statement (IPS). Your IPS is a critical first step in building a structure for asset management. It defines your preferred investments based on your level of acceptable decline, and determines the strategy that will best meet these objectives. This serves as a framework for allocating assets among various investment classes.

The IPS will help you identify your risk tolerance level so that you can weather the inevitable downturns in the market. It's only through long-term planning that you are going to be successful and not be waylaid by common pitfalls. In the heat of a bull market, it is critical to have a well thought out strategy far in advance of the time it's needed. As we move through the workbook, we will be answering questions and filling in your IPS.

EXHIBIT I-1 How to Use This Workbook

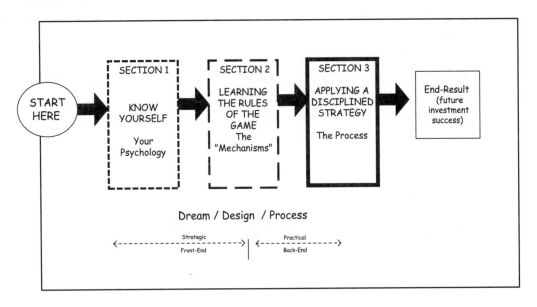

HOW THIS WORKBOOK IS ORGANIZED

Section One introduces you to all the basic steps you'll need to follow in order to benefit the most from this book. It focuses primarily on knowing yourself, and understanding your needs and constraints. You will learn about your investing temperament. You may know your financial needs, but not your personal dynamics or what sort of tolerances you have. That should no longer be true after completing this section.

These factors are particularly important to incorporate into your decision making. In planning a trip or your financial future some people will say speed is the most important factor. For others, arriving safely is the highest priority. Still others will decide that cost is most important. These differences determine how you will travel and how fast you'll get there.

Section Two covers the rules of the game. This is the more complicated part, but we have sought to streamline and simplify the concepts we will be presenting and give you the tools you will need to implement your plan.

Section Three explains how to successfully apply a disciplined investment strategy and implement what you have learned to successfully chart a course for your investment future.

CAUTION—Don't let the title "first time investor" confuse you. There are several scenarios that would qualify someone as a first time investor. For instance, you'd be surprised at the number of investors who have thought they were investing, but who were really speculating. These people are actually first time investors. You can be rich and be a first time investor; or you could have been investing for years without proper guidance and consistently losing money, and now you want to become an informed investor.

This workbook is designed for the person who has been saving for a number of years, or who has money in a 401(k) plan, or who has somehow ended up with $50,000 or more. Or, someone who has not yet started a savings program but is looking to the future and wants to determine how much money he or she will need for retirement.

SPECIAL FEATURES OF THIS WORKBOOK

Follow the ICONS—they can make your job easier: Alongside the text of this workbook, you will find several different pictures that are used to inform, warn, emphasize, or alert you to special opportunities.

ACTION—The following are actions you should take, fill in, or complete. These are the crucial steps needed to complete your IPS.

TECHNICAL—You may feel this is a bit too much technical information. These are sections you may want to read again. These concepts will help with your understanding.

IDEA—Here is a little extra information that can help you avoid a problem or take advantage of an opportunity. The idea may save you money, time, and trouble.

EASY TO UNDERSTAND—Just as the name suggests, this icon indicates concepts that are particularly simple to understand.

CAUTION—Don't make a mistake that can cost you money or get you off your investment path. This icon will help you stay out of trouble.

YOUR FINANCIAL RISKOMETER—The risk level you can expect from an investment or investment strategy. This icon will tell you what to expect or to watch out for.

LIFE SITUATION—You may have a special situation in your family: kids going to college, a divorce, or a death.

GETTING STARTED

As you begin this process we want to prepare you for the work ahead. We have sought to streamline the educational process so you learn vital information in a simple, practical, and fun manner.

Our goal is to ensure that by the time you have finished this book you will have learned to use some practical and useful tools that will help guide you to success in the financial portion of your life.

The cornerstone of this process will be your personal investment policy statement (IPS) that is included in this section. As you work through this book, you will be completing your IPS. This will serve as your road map to success. It will be a tool that you can use for the rest of your life and adjust as needs change.

As we work through this, let's make sure that you remember a couple of very important rules.

First, be honest and objective. Investing is very personal and so there are no universal right answers to many of these questions. However, as you work through this, the more objective you can be, the higher quality the end-result will be. Err on the side of being conservative; fear is a much stronger emotion than greed. If you are giving conservative answers, you will at least be prepared when your investments test your resolve (yes, that will happen).

Second, be patient. Don't rush. This is a lifelong journey. If you learn only one thing from this book, we hope it is that being well-prepared and being patient will put you in the best position to succeed.

Third, keep it simple. The financial services industry has thrived on keeping things very complicated. Don't think that the more academic the answer, the better it is. As you go through this process and beyond, always remember to look at any opportunity in the context of your plan (the IPS). It is our hope that you will benefit hugely from the journey you are about to embark on.

Following are the seven steps you will be taking through the course of this book. After that is the IPS that will become your investment road map. We will be completing it throughout the book. Please use a pencil (your answers will change over time). Then we get going in earnest. Enjoy!

A Checklist of the Seven Steps to Success

Check the boxes as you complete these steps.

❏ Review IPS.

❏ Follow action steps in Section One to complete investor profile (A,B,C) in the IPS.

❏ Read the rest of Section One and follow action steps to complete questions 1 to 6 in the IPS.

❏ Review Section Two.

❏ Must read the five rules and six concepts in Section Two.

❏ Read Section Three and follow action steps to complete questions 7 and 8 of the IPS.

❏ Implement your strategy with an advisor or alone.

THE INVESTMENT POLICY STATEMENT (IPS)

Following are your IPSs for your three categories of money. We'll be going into detail on how to complete these over the course of the workbook. Use a pencil.

A. What life stage are you in? _____

B. How much money will you need? And in which of these buckets? _____

_____

   Short-term   How much money have you allocated to short-term? _____

_____

   Mid-term   How much money have you allocated to mid-term? _____

_____

   Long-term   How much money have you allocated to long-term? _____

_____

C. What kind of investor are you? _____

SHORT-TERM—INCIDENTAL EVERYDAY MONEY

1. What level of decline can you tolerate? The lifeboat drill _____ % _____

2. What is your time horizon? (Typically, from 0 to 18 months)_____

3. What are your liquidity needs?   High ❑   Medium ❑   Low ❑

4. What is your tax rate on underlying investments? (Federal Tax Rate Guide) _____

_____

5. Any legal considerations? _____

6. Any unique circumstances? _____

7. What is a reasonable growth rate? _____

8. What investments are appropriate? _____

_____

_____

MID-TERM—MAJOR PURCHASE MONEY
(HOUSE, COLLEGE, WEDDINGS, ETC.)

1. What level of decline can you tolerate? The lifeboat drill _____ % _____

2. What is your time horizon? (Typically, 18 months to 5 years) _____

3. What are your liquidity needs?   High ❑   Medium ❑   Low ❑

4. What is your tax rate on underlying investments? (Federal Tax Rate Guide) _____

_____

5. Any legal considerations? _____

6. Any unique circumstances? _____

7. What is a reasonable growth rate? _____

8. What investments are appropriate? _____

_____

_____

LONG-TERM—RETIREMENT MONEY

1. What level of decline can you tolerate? The lifeboat drill _____ % _____

2. What is your time horizon? (Typically, 5 to 20 years) _____

3. What are your liquidity needs?   High ❑   Medium ❑   Low ❑

4. What is your tax rate on underlying investments? (Federal Tax Rate Guide) _____

5. Any legal considerations? _____

6. Any unique circumstances? _____

7. What is a reasonable growth rate? _____

8. What investments are appropriate? _____

_____

_____

THE FINANCIAL SUCCESS DIET

Think of investing as you think of dieting. With investments, just as with food, we sometimes crave what is not good for us. Maybe we love to eat chocolate or an extra slice of buttered bread, although we know that eating these foods will not help us lose weight. Investing is not that different. Often, we are tempted by an exciting investment and we ignore risk and succumb to greed. Giving in to this temptation will make you as unsuccessful in investing as you would be in dieting if you ate a candy bar whenever you felt the urge to do so.

Suppose your goal is to lose 25 pounds. There are many trendy approaches to choose from. But, every fad comes and goes, and the main beneficiaries are the marketers of those fads.

Say you've decided to follow a popular high-protein diet that prohibits eating any starches, chocolate, or sugar. You have a sweet tooth and if you don't eat your candy bar every afternoon, you won't get through the day. How likely is it that you're going to stick to this diet? You're probably going to return to that daily candy bar within two weeks, even after you've lost your first 10 pounds. And what happens after you start eating that daily candy bar again? You'll forget about the discipline that helped you lose the 10 pounds. Two months later you'll be back where you were before, having had only a temporary weight loss.

If you know yourself and factor that knowledge into the dieting process, you will be able to ensure that you choose a disciplined long-term plan you can stick to. The investing process is very similar.

If you're going to be successful at losing weight, it's not just about going on the diet-of-the-day, taking up aerobics, or giving up sugar. You must first understand your own makeup, your own desires and needs, and what you are comfortable doing. Then, when presented with an alternative, you can decide whether it fits into your plan.

If you want to lose weight and somebody shows you the high-protein diet, you might think *"I really don't like steak, but maybe I could take a couple of these ideas and incorporate them into my diet plan."* The same is true of investing. If you have a structured plan and you understand who you are and what you want your investments to accomplish for you, when you hear of a new idea, you can evaluate it in the context of your whole plan and see how it might play a role. Then it's not just a random reaction.

You won't be like the people who join a fitness club, only to find after their first session, and the resulting sore muscles, that it's not for them—and the only long-term result they get is paying off their contract. The only thing that gets thin is their wallet.

There is no shortcut or magic pill. You need to understand the rules of the game and plan a good strategy based on your financial goals and how much money you'll require to meet them.

To achieve your desired weight loss, you can try to do it on your own, or you can hire a personal trainer to whom you're accountable. A personal trainer will check your diet, guide your workout, make sure you're staying healthy, and correct any mistakes you make. In the investing process, a financial planner will do the same for your financial health and well being.

We want to stress the importance of being well educated and of understanding yourself and the rules of the game prior to deciding whether to work with an advisor or do it yourself. If you choose to work with a financial planner, your knowledge will help you select the right person and keep you from being taken advantage of, and will allow the relationship between planner and client to become a truly mentoring one.

Whether you choose to work alone or with an advisor, following this process will give you *control* and *understanding*—the two key elements to being successful. When you go on a diet, you know how much weight you want to lose. When you start an investment program, you need to know your financial goals and how much money you're going to need to meet them.

MENTAL ACCOUNTING

Mental accounting is the process of compartmentalizing your investments. This is something most people do automatically. What does this mean? It means that we place certain pools of money in different categories in our minds. Imagine that you have a closet full of clothes. You place your "going out" clothes in one area, your work clothes in another, and then you compartmentalize your "going out" clothes into casual and dressy areas. You may or may not have physically partitioned out your clothes that way; however, in your mind you have almost certainly placed certain clothing items in each category.

This is true of investing, and yet, many people do not have a rational way of structuring their mental compartments for their money. This type of thinking ends up in a hodgepodge of investment results—the primary one being that people feel no sense of control. They have no disciplined way to look at problems as they arise. They find themselves disorganized, unprepared, and even worse, making crucial mistakes that can be easily avoided.

Many people keep a portion of their "just in case" money in CDs while they borrow on their credit cards. If you do this, you are borrowing money at a very high interest rate (the average credit card charges 16 percent interest) and then lending it to the bank at a much lower one (about 6 percent). In this case you are actually paying 10 percent a year for every dollar you have in CDs that you also owe in credit cards. This doesn't include the fact that you have to pay taxes on your CD rate and will not receive any tax break on credit card debt. The end result? The banks do great, you don't.

We recommend that you take these mental compartments and put them on paper where you can divide your money into three major components: short-term, mid-term, and long-term. These components have unique time horizons (the range of time over which you will need this money), and, as you will see, this will determine the risk you can take and the investments that are appropriate for you.

Let's define the three categories of money you need in your life:

- **Short-Term—Incidental Everyday Money.** This is money you need for everyday use; for example, paying bills, buying clothes, or taking vacations. You need your short-term money to be absolutely risk-free because you're going to need it in the present or near future. The time horizon on this portion of money is typically from the present to 18 months in the future.

- **Mid-Term—Major Purchase Money.** Major purchases include buying a home, a car, paying for a son or daughter's wedding, major medical expenses, and so forth. For most major purchases, the time horizon will be 18 months to 5 years.

- **Long-Term—Retirement Money.** What do you have set up for retirement? We will take a piece of your money and develop a business plan and call it your retirement nest egg. Everyone needs long-term money. Even the people who have already retired need long-term money. A typical time horizon is 5 to 10 years.

To assist in this process, we're going to refer to each of these investment pools as "buckets."

WHAT LIFESTYLE STAGE ARE YOU IN?

The percentage of money you will allocate to each of these investment categories generally correlates to certain life stages (Exhibit 1-1).

EXHIBIT 1-1 Risk/Return Positions in the Life-Cycle Stages

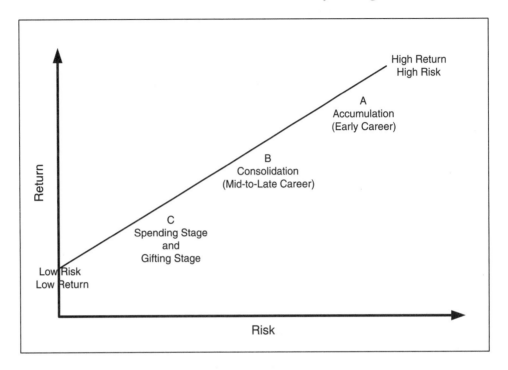

Is your mix of short-term, mid-term, and long-term investments in range with the phase of life you're in? Let us show you what percentage of net worth people typically have in each of these three categories in each of the major lifestyle stages.

Accumulation Phase

Age range is usually 25 to 45. At this stage you are primarily in your earning and spending period. You have a lot of short-term money that is being earned and spent. Priorities are mostly goal oriented or mid-term in nature and they include saving for children's education, a larger home, life and disability insurance, and, if possible, investments for future financial independence. Long-term assets are typically either nondiversified, with home equity the largest asset, or illiquid to the point of inaccessibility in the form of employee retirement programs. With a long time horizon, you can undertake more high-return, high-risk capital gain–oriented investments with your long-term money. You should be saving as much as you can into your long-term assets since, with time on your side, every dollar can grow significantly.

As we begin to save, most of our assets are in short-term and mid-term vehicles because we have high current expenses and a lot of goal-oriented mid-term expenses. Long-term savings are almost always in the form of some retirement account.

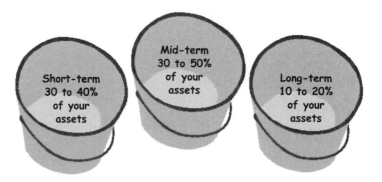

If you're young, it's not going to take a lot of capital or effort to build a substantial retirement account. Exhibit 1-2 will show you starting ages, rates of return you'd need, and the amount you'd have to invest to have a million dollars at retirement. It's not impossible!

Consolidation Phase

Age range is usually 45 to 65. The consolidation or mid-to-late-career stage of the typical life cycle is characterized by the period when income exceeds expenses; typically, after children have left home or after the need for larger homes and more things to fill them has finally become sated. Short-term income often exceeds needs; mid-term goals are diminished somewhat and

EXHIBIT 1-2 How to Have a Million at Age 65

Starting Age	AMOUNT YOU HAVE TO INVEST PER MONTH		
	8% Return	10% Return	15% Return
25	$310	$180	$45
30	$470	$300	$90
35	$710	$490	$180
40	$1,100	$810	$370
45	$1,760	$1,390	$760
50	$2,960	$2,500	$1,640
55	$5,550	$5,000	$3,850
60	$13,700	$13,050	$11,600

Source: The First Time Investor by Larry Chambers (McGraw-Hill, 1999).

retirement planning becomes the primary goal. This stage is characterized by the accumulation and growth of an investment portfolio. Home equity and retirement program benefits are becoming substantial as well. At the same time, the time horizon to retirement and beyond is still relatively long (10 to 20 years).

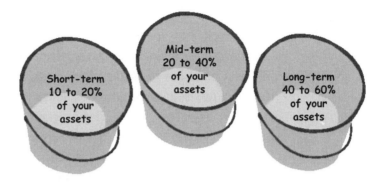

At this stage is when earnings are typically maximized and so there is very little need for additional short-term income. We have mid-term money for certain goals and peace of mind. Long-term savings should become a major component of our asset mix.

Spending Phase

Age range is usually 60 to 75. The "spending phase" is defined here as the period when one is financially independent: that is, living expenses are covered not from earned income but from accumulated assets such as investments and retirement programs. There is a heavy reliance on personal investments, and a focus on assets with relatively secure values, with more emphasis on dividend, interest, and rental income. Of course, the individual's time horizon may still be well over 10 to 20 years (even an 80-year-old has a life expectancy of 9.5 more years), so some investments in the portfolio should continue to have growth and inflation-hedge potential.

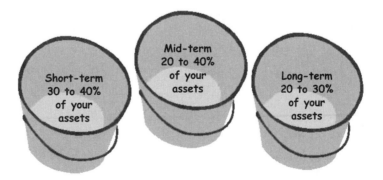

As we retire, we need to shift our assets to cover our short-term expenses for the next year and safety becomes increasingly important. There should be a significant portion still allocated to long-term growth. This mix shifts with more assets going to the shorter term as we stay longer into retirement.

Gifting Phase

The final life cycle stage of gifting occurs when the individual comes to realize that he or she has more assets than will ever be needed for personal spending and personal security. Risk/return preference may not be different from the previous stage, but attitudes about the purpose of investments do change.

The asset mix clearly depends on the size of the gift. Typically, assets to be gifted should be invested in a tax-sensitive manner if they are in a taxable trust, and invested for growth if they are in a nontaxable trust. However, this is very dependent on the beneficiaries' needs.

You may find that you do not fall clearly into one of these phases—there may be some overlap. Obviously, your goals will vary depending on your life-cycle phase. You should be guided more by the description of the phases than by the age ranges. Which phase are you in?

What lifestyle stage are you in?

❑ Accumulating

❑ Consolidating

❑ Spending

❑ Gifting

 Go to the IPS on page 7 and fill in question A by indicating your lifestyle stage.

HOW MUCH MONEY WILL YOU NEED?

Think of each of the three categories as a bucket of money: you have the short-term bucket, mid-term bucket, long-term bucket. Examine your investments. How much money have you allocated to each of these buckets? Is that amount consistent with the stage of life you're in? Maybe there need to be some adjustments made.

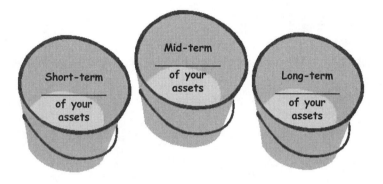

NOTES: _____

_____

_____

_____

If your mix doesn't match with the guidelines we've discussed, you might want to consider moving more money to those areas in which you have less. If you don't want to make that shift, you probably have a good reason. For example, if you're in the accumulation phase and you have a lot less of your net worth in short-term money, it is probably because you generate a lot of short-term income; for example, you may receive a large salary. You can therefore afford to save a much bigger portion of your money than is typical of somebody in your stage of life.

 Determine a percentage amount for each pool of money. You can calculate what percent of your total net worth is currently allocated to different buckets. First add up all three pools of money; then divide each one by the total of the three.

Your numbers are going to be different. For example, if you have $10,000 in the first bucket, $50,000 in the second, and $100,000 in the third bucket, the total amount would be $160,000. Divide $10,000 by $160,000 to find what percentage of your total net worth is in your short-term bucket (16 percent), and so on.

Next, knowing what you've learned about yourself, decide if this mix is the best. Do you believe you are putting enough into the retirement bucket? If not, add more to it.

- **Short-Term**—How much money have you allocated to short-term?

  Our example: $10,000; yours: _____

- **Mid-Term**—How much money have you allocated to mid-term?

  Our example: $50,000; yours: _____

- **Long-Term**—How much money have you allocated to long-term?

  Our example: $100,000; yours: _____

Obviously, as you get older, your major acquisitions diminish somewhat. Once you retire, your retirement money starts to move over to the mid-term and short-term categories. If you've already retired, take a piece of your retirement money and allocate it to your five year money; take another piece of your money and allocate it to your current needs money, but keep a piece of it in your long-term bucket.

Go to the IPS on page 7 and fill in amounts for each bucket of money in question B.

How much money will you put into each of these buckets?

- Short-term bucket $ _____

- Mid-term bucket $ _____

- Long-term bucket $ _____

WHAT KIND OF INVESTOR ARE YOU?

The following model was created by researchers Bailard, Biehl & Kaiser (BB&K)[1] to help classify investor personalities by focusing on two aspects of personality: the level of confidence and the method of action.

The first deals with how confidently you approach life. These are important emotional choices, and they are dictated by how confident you are about some things or how much you tend to worry about them.

The second element deals with whether you are methodical, careful, and analytical in your approach to life or whether you are emotional, intuitive, and impetuous.

These two elements can be thought of as two "axes" of individual psychology; one axis is called the "confident–anxious" axis, and the other is called the "careful–impetuous" axis (or the compulsive–impulsive axis). You should recognize yourself in one (or more) of the following personality profiles (Exhibit 1-3).

The profiles will help you to determine whether you would benefit from working with an advisor or not.

EXHIBIT 1-3 Investor Personality Characteristics

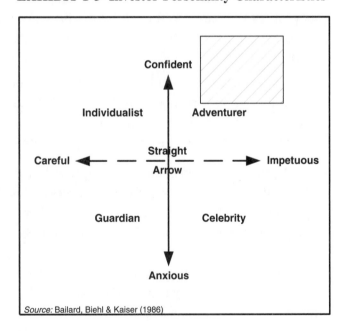

Source: Bailard, Biehl & Kaiser (1986)

---

[1]A paper from The Institute of Chartered Financial Analysts, page 37.

The Five Personalities

Adventurers. The upper-right-hand area of the figure represents adventurers—people who are willing to put everything in one major bet and "go for it" because they have confidence and trust their instincts. In that quadrant, one typically finds entrepreneurs and people who are willing to stick their necks out in their careers or in their money management strategies.

Celebrities. The lower-right-hand quadrant represents celebrities. These are people who like to be where the action is. They are afraid of being left out. They are often enticed by the latest investment fad and are subject to a follow-the-herd mentality.

Individualists. The individualists are in the upper-left-hand quadrant. These people tend to go their own way and are typified by the small-business person or an independent professional such as a lawyer, CPA, or engineer. These are people who are out trying to make their own decisions in life. They have a certain degree of confidence about their decisions but are also careful, methodical, and analytical.

Guardians. The lower-left-hand quadrant represents the guardian personality. Guardians have less confidence than individualists and make up for it by being extremely cautious and deliberate. Typically, as people get older and begin considering retirement, they approach this personality profile. They are careful and a little bit worried about their money. They recognize that they face a limited earning time span and have to preserve their assets.

Straight-Arrows. Finally, there are always people who are so balanced that they cannot be placed in any specific quadrant, so they fall near the center. These investors are called straight-arrow people. However, most of these folks still have a slight leaning toward one of the other four types.

A guardian can become more aggressive for a time, like an adventurer, if he or she is on a winning streak. Conversely, most investors become more guardian-like just after an event like the October 1987 stock market crash. As time passes, people tend to shift into more conservative areas, or shift further left.

Experience has shown that each of the five types of investors requires a different approach in investing (Exhibit 1-4). A few guidelines and cautions follow:

- If you are an adventurer, you are typically entrepreneurial and strong-willed. You have your own ideas about investing. You are willing to take risks, and you prefer concentrating your bets. A well-diversified approach is often boring for you. You might decide, for example, that the next big

EXHIBIT 1-4 Investor Personality Do-It-Yourselfers

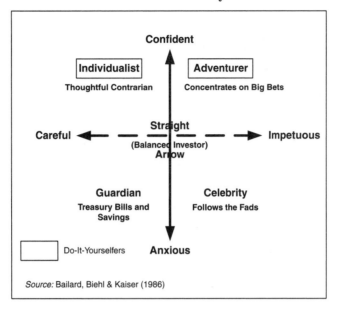

Source: Bailard, Biehl & Kaiser (1986)

move in the market will be in small-cap stocks, and you would hire a small-cap specialist. At a later time, you might decide that the next big move will be in real estate, at which point you would hire a real estate specialist. You are a true do-it-yourself investor, although you might consider working with an advisor in order to diversify some of your decision making.

- If you're a celebrity, you know what's in style in the investment world and you follow the popular fashion. You don't want to be left out of the latest hot investment. Celebrities may have their own ideas about other things in life, but not about investing. As a result, they are easy prey for maximum turnover brokers who spin the next great story. If you work with an advisor, you will probably be drawn in by the latest trend, and that leaves you vulnerable to be taken advantage of. Celebrity investors are often hurt by investing in trends too late.

- An individualist investor is independent and tends to be skeptical in nature. Individualists approach investing with a contrarian view and are self-directed and confident in their decision-making skills. They work with an advisor to implement a strategy they believe in, but they do not like to be told what to do. If you choose to work with an advisor, you should work with an advisor who can implement your plan in accordance with your desires and who is not intent on selling you the latest trend. This type of investor is very meticulous and desires a consistent approach to investing.

- On the other hand, if you are a guardian, you are highly loss-averse and are cautiously trying to preserve your wealth. You are definitely not interested in volatility or excitement. Guardians lack confidence in their ability to forecast the future or to understand where to put money, so they look for guidance. They tend to be very careful about selecting an investment advisor, but once they have chosen someone, they are often intensely loyal. If you are this type of investor, you are not alone. This seems to be where most people fall when it comes to styles of money management. In 401(k) or profit-sharing plans in which individuals have a choice of how to allocate their money, they sometimes will allocate a little more of their portfolio to whatever is currently hot. But mostly, they allocate a fairly high proportion of their money to money market funds, guaranteed investment contracts, or balanced funds.

- Or are you a straight-arrow type? If so, you do not fall into any of the personality extremes of the individualist, adventurer, celebrity, or guardian. This group represents the average investor, a relatively balanced composite of each of the other four investor types, and, by implication, a group willing to be exposed to medium amounts of risk. Typically, even the straight-arrow investor has a tilt toward one of the other four types.

Given the various individual investor types discussed, and where you fit, how are you likely to carry out your proposed investment program?

Adventurers and individualist investor types are often do-it-yourselfers. The individualists are the thoughtful contrarians. The adventurers concentrate on big bets.

Celebrities often follow the herd and benefit from quality advice; however, they often succumb to a great "story." Finally, the largest portion of investors is shown in the boxed area of Exhibit 1-5. These investors tend to be heavily oriented toward the typical guardian personality. They are often people who have made their money and are not willing to put it at risk, sometimes to their own detriment, as they struggle to keep ahead of taxes and inflation. Working with a knowledgeable and risk-conscious advisor can have a significant impact on their portfolios.

All the different types of investors can choose to work alone or with advisors. In Section Three we will provide specific recommendations for the kind of advisor you should work with, or if you choose to go it alone, some warnings as to what to watch out for.

Inherited Wealth

Inheritors can be very risk-averse because, not having earned the wealth themselves, they may be very fearful about what they would do without it.

EXHIBIT 1-5 Investor Personality Investment Counsel Clientele

Confident

Individualist   Adventurer

Careful ←----------- **Straight** -----------→ Impetuous
                      (Balanced Investor)
                      Arrow

Guardian   Celebrity

[ ] Investment Counsel
      Clientele   **Anxious**

Source: Bailard, Biehl & Kaiser (1986)

The best advice for you if you have inherited wealth, is to educate yourself about investment options as well as the psychology of inheritance. There are many issues that someone who inherits wealth needs to confront.

Identify which type of investor you are and check the box. ***Then go to the IPS on page 7 and complete question C.***

❏ *Adventurer*

❏ *Celebrity*

❏ *Individualist*

❏ *Guardian*

❏ *Straight-Arrow*

THE LIFEBOAT DRILL

What Level of Decline Can You Tolerate?

Risk can be measured in many ways. Most institutions use a measurement called *beta* to measure market risk.

 Beta is a measure of the risk of an investment compared to that of the market. This is a good way to measure risk; however, it is often not very useful for individuals since individuals don't look at risk in relative terms. Your risk is the chance that you are not going to have the money you need when you need it.

Far more important for the individual is how much absolute decline they are willing to risk in their portfolio. Since most investors facing a significant loss in their portfolios make shifts to preserve them by moving to cash or another safe alternative, it is important to know what *your* risk tolerance is in each of the three categories of money and that you invest appropriately.

In the following exercise, you will measure your risk tolerance for each of the three buckets of money we've identified. In the next few pages we are going to put together an investment policy for the three different investment pools. We have shaded the risk profile most common for each investment pool; however your risk profile might be different.

As you complete this exercise, you should consider that when investing in stocks or other risky investments, it's likely you will experience twice the volatility of the expected growth.

What does that mean? If you're investing to capture 10 percent growth in a fully invested portfolio, you can expect to experience about twice that in decline every three to five years or so. If you're looking for a 15 percent growth on a whole portfolio, fully invested, you can expect declines in the range of 30 percent every three to five years or so.

Mistakes First Time Investors Make

 A mistake many first time investors make is to look at risk the way institutions do. Institutions use relative performance to measure risk, but this measure isn't really relevant to you, the individual.

If a mutual fund has a beta of 0.8, it is said to be 80 percent as risky as the stock market. Therefore, if the stock market was down 20 percent, and your mutual fund had a beta of 0.8, that mutual fund should be down 16 percent (or 80 percent of 20 percent).

For an institutional investor, if that mutual fund was down less than 16 percent, it has *outperformed*. However, for us as individual investors, we might not necessarily feel that way. That's the difference between an individual and an institution. Institutional tools aren't always helpful to you.

Most investors do not care about relative performance; they care only about absolute performance—about what actually happens with their money.

On the next few pages are sample worksheets for each of the three categories of investments: short-, mid-, and long-term. We have shaded the areas that are most common for each investment, but you should still do what is most appropriate for you. Concentrate not on the percentages, but on the dollar amounts.

Use the space provided to answer the questions for your circumstances in each of the categories. Then review the risk table and fill in how much decline you could accept, both in dollar amounts and in percentages.

It is very important that you answer these questions honestly, as they will form the cornerstone of your investment strategy. Be sure to include in your decision making anyone else who might be relevant to the process, for example, your spouse or heirs.

The Drills

Assume, as in our example, that you have $160,000 divided into your three money buckets. In the first month, your investments all go up 3 percent. You feel pretty good, right? In the next month, everything goes up 2 percent. You're feeling even better, right? But what if your money starts to decline? Your ship is taking on water—how low in the water will you let the boat sink before you abandon ship?

Let's now go through the drill with the three different pools of money. When do you jump into the lifeboat with your short-term money? Assume you have $10,000 in short-term cash.

Short-Term Money Drill

Read down Exhibit 1-6 until you come to a place where you feel the decline is unacceptable and you would get into your lifeboat. Place a check mark in the appropriate box. You will notice that we shaded the 3 percent area. Why? Because this money is needed day-by-day and at a moment's notice. An investor should not be willing to accept too many movements with this money.

 Place a check mark in the appropriate box. We've shaded the area most appropriate.

EXHIBIT 1-6 Short-Term Money Drill

Potential Quarterly Decline	Original Investment $10,000	Check the Box Where You Would Take Action
(3%)	$9,700	☐
(6%)	$9,400	☐
(8%)	$9,200	☐
(10%)	$9,000	☐
(15%)	$8,500	☐
(23%)	$7,700	☐
(35%)	$6,500	☐
(50%)	$5,000	☐

NOTES: _____

_____

_____

_____

_____

_____

Mid-Term Money Drill

Assume you have $50,000 dedicated for mid-term money you'll need in the next 18 months to 3 years. Read down Exhibit 1-7 until you come to a place where you feel the decline is unacceptable and you would get into your lifeboat.

 Place a check mark in the appropriate box. We've shaded the area most appropriate.

EXHIBIT 1-7 Mid-Term Money Drill

Potential Quarterly Decline	Original Investment $50,000	Check the Box Where You Would Take Action
(3%)	$48,500	☐
(6%)	$47,000	☐
(8%)	$46,000	☐
(10%)	$45,000	☐
(15%)	$42,500	☐
(23%)	$38,500	☐
(35%)	$32,500	☐
(50%)	$25,000	☐

NOTES: _____

_____

_____

_____

_____

_____

Long-Term Money Drill

Assume you have $100,000 dedicated for long-term money. On your next monthly statement, you see that your $100,000 has become $97,000. Are you still on board? Next month, you're down to $94,000. Then it drops to $92,000. How are you feeling now? Are you still okay with doing nothing or are you getting your lifeboat ready? The month after that, it drops to $90,000. Then it goes down further to $85,000, $77,000, $65,000, and eventually to $50,000. At what point do you jump ship?

 Read down Exhibit 1-8 until you come to a place where you feel the decline is unacceptable and you would get into your lifeboat. Place a check mark in the appropriate box.

EXHIBIT 1-8 Long-Term Money Drill

Potential Quarterly Decline	Original Investment $100,000	Check the Box Where You Would Take Action
(3%)	$97,000	☐
(6%)	$94,000	☐
(8%)	$92,000	☐
(10%)	$90,000	☐
(15%)	$85,000	☐
(23%)	$77,000	☐
(35%)	$65,000	☐
(50%)	$50,000	☐

NOTES: _____

_____

_____

_____

On your $100,000, you might be willing to endure a 3 percent decline; you probably aren't very willing to sit still at a 5 percent drop; and at a 15 percent drop, nearly everybody wants out. Isn't it interesting that you are willing to accept a greater percentage amount when it isn't related to a specific dollar amount?

We react more strongly to dollar amounts than we do to percentages. To demonstrate this, cover up the dollar amounts and repeat the exercise looking only at the percentages. Percentages are the financial service industry's equivalent of casino gambling chips. By abstracting money into chips or percentages, the impact of loss is lessened for the gambler or for the investor.

 Go to your IPS on pages 7–9 and fill in question 1 for each of the three money drills.

1. What level of decline can you tolerate?

    ❑ Short-term quarterly decline _____%   ❑ Dollar amount of decline $ _____

    ❑ Mid-term quarterly decline _____%   ❑ Dollar amount of decline $ _____

    ❑ Long-term quarterly decline _____ %   ❑ Dollar amount of decline $ _____

RECOGNIZING YOUR CONSTRAINTS

Once you determine your investment objectives, they must be balanced with your constraints as an investor. Constraints are measured by your time horizon. They are also measured against liquidity considerations on your money, tax issues, and unique circumstances such as estates, charitable giving, and divorce.

WHAT IS YOUR TIME HORIZON?

Your time horizon is typically one of your constraints. Since you've already sorted your money into three pools, your horizons have been broken out into three different investment types.

- Short-term time horizon   _____ Months (Typically, from 0 to 18 months)

- Mid-term time horizon   _____ Months/years (Typically, 18 months to 5 years)

- Long-term time horizon   _____ Years (Typically 5 to 20 years)

NOTES: _____

_____

_____

_____

_____

_____

Go to your IPS on pages 7–9 and fill in the time horizon in question 2 for each of the three money drills.

LIQUIDITY

Liquidity is your need for current cash from your investments. Typically, your need for liquidity in the short-term will be high, your need in the mid-term will be medium, and your need in the long-term will be low. As you get closer to retirement, more of your net worth will be in the medium bucket, which will automatically tell you that you have medium needs for liquidity. Liquidity needs are going to be high to moderate when you've retired.

NOTES: _____

_____

_____

_____

_____

_____

Go to your IPS on pages 7–9 and indicate if your liquidity need is high, medium, or low in question 3 for each of the three money drills.

TAX RATES

What is your tax rate on anything that you realize gains on? If you're investing for longer than 12 months, you really want to do whatever you can to defer taxes, because there is a big difference between paying long-term and short-term taxes on your investments.

Determine your federal and state tax rates. Exhibit 1-9 shows you the current federal rates. Remember that long-term gains are taxed at a lower rate. Also note that any money in a retirement plan such as an IRA or a 401(k) is not taxed as long as it stays invested.

EXHIBIT 1-9 Federal Tax Rates

Schedule X - filing single
If taxable income is

Over	But not over	The tax is	Of the amount over
$ 0	$ 25,750	15%	$ 0
25,750	62,450	$3,862.50 + 28%	25,750
62,450	130,250	14,138.50 + 31%	62,450
130,250	283,150	35,156.50 + 36%	130,250
283,150		90,200.50 + 39.6%	283,150

Schedule Y-1 - Married, filing jointly of Qualified Widow(er)
If taxable income is

Over	But not over	The tax is	Of the amount over
$ 0	$ 43,050	15%	$ 0
43,050	104,050	$6,457.50 + 28%	43,050
104,050	158,550	23,537.50 + 31%	104,050
158,550	283,150	40,432.50 + 36%	158,550
283,150		85,288.50 + 39.6%	283,150

Schedule Y-2 - Married, filing separately
If taxable income is

Over	But not over	The tax is	Of the amount over
$ 0	$ 21,525	15%	$ 0
21,525	52,025	$3,228.75 + 28%	21,525
52,025	79,275	11,768.75 + 31%	52,025
79,275	141,575	20,216.25 + 36%	79,275
141,575		42,644.25 + 39.6%	141,575

Schedule Z - Head of Household
If taxable income is

Over	But not over	The tax is	Of the amount over
$ 0	$ 34,550	15%	$ 0
34,550	89,150	$5,182.50 + 28%	34,500
89,150	144,400	20,470.50 + 31%	89,150
144,400	283,150	37,598.00 + 36%	144,400
283,150		87,548.00 + 39.6%	283,150

NOTES: _____

_____

_____

_____

 Go to your IPS on pages 7–9 and write in your tax rate in question 4 for each of the three money drills.

Federal and State Tax Rates

Adjusted Gross Income (AGI). Total earned and unearned income from taxable accounts, including net business income or losses, capital gain or loss, retirement plan distributions, taxable pensions, rental income, and possibly some Social Security benefits, minus IRA, SEP, or Keogh contributions, self-employment health benefits (partially deductible so far), half your self-employment tax, and alimony paid. The AGI is the last line on the front of Form 1040.

Taxable Income. The AGI minus personal exemptions and itemized or standard deduction. This is the figure on which you calculate your tax.

Capital Gain or Loss. This is the difference between what an investment sells for and its tax-cost basis, and any combination and fees for buying and/or selling. A mutual fund or real estate investment trust (REIT) may declare capital gain dividends to shareholders on the same basis.

Alternative Minimum Tax (AMT). The AMT was created to make sure that wealthy people with a lot of fancy deductions and credits paid a reasonable minimum tax. But now it may affect single filers with a taxable income of $33,750 or more and married taxpayers with incomes over $45,000. It's really a set of entirely different tax rules that affects millions of middle-class taxpayers who have high deductions or tax credits in certain areas. There's no simple way to figure out if it applies to you unless you do the calculations. If you don't calculate it, the IRS will. And if it applies to you, look out!

LEGAL CONSIDERATIONS

Are There Any Legal Considerations?

- Is this money in a trust or a 401(k)?

- Are there any unique circumstances such as a charity you want to contribute to, or specific goals you need to accomplish with the money?

NOTES: _____

_____

_____

_____

_____

_____

 Go to your IPS on pages 7–9 and write any legal considerations in question 5 for each of the three money drills.

UNIQUE CIRCUMSTANCES

Do you have any unique circumstances that you should mention for each of the three pools of money? It is quite possible that you have no legal considerations or unique circumstances in your short-term money. But if you have your long-term money in a 401(k), there are legal considerations or unique circumstances on that piece of your portfolio.

Answer each of these questions for each of the three categories.

NOTES: _____

_____

_____

_____

_____

_____

 Go to your IPS on pages 7–9 and write any unique circumstances in question 6 for each of the three money drills. We will complete questions 7 and 8 in Section Three.

You now should be armed with the knowledge of who you are as an investor.

Next, we turn to Section Two, which is broken into two parts: Part One is a must-do because these are the general rules and concepts of investing and investment axioms that everyone has to know. Part Two is optional, but it gives you much more detail about different investment styles and classes. We recommend that you read it.

In Section Three, we show you how to apply your knowledge and finish your IPS. Then, as a reference guide so you can see how it's working, we'll show you some real-world examples of people in each of the life phases and how they use these tools.

RECAP

Before we move on, let's take a quick inventory:

Do you feel that you've learned more about yourself? _____ Yes _____ No

Do you feel that you have a better understanding about how to compartmentalize your money? _____ Yes _____ No

What lifestyle stage are you in? _____

What personality type are you? _____

Have you completed questions A, B, and C of your IPS on pages 7–9? _____ Yes _____ No

Have you completed the first six questions for each of the money drills on pages 7–9 of your IPS? _____ Yes _____ No

Are you a more informed investor? _____ Yes _____ No

Now let's move on and learn *the rules of the game!*

SECTION TWO

THE RULES OF THE GAME

This section's focus is on understanding the rules of investing. This is an educational process. We're going to introduce you to some sophisticated tools, but we'll do so in a simple way that's easy and fun to follow. It's a structured, proven, systematic process that works. If you read nothing more than the five rules and six concepts in this section, you will have at least gotten the basic information crucial to your investment success.

There are many alternatives in investing, and there are trade-offs in each investing scenario. This section is designed to help you to understand the trade-offs so you can make informed decisions. This is the homework section. If you do not understand the various investments and how they work together, it is very difficult to put together a successful investment strategy.

As you go through this section, you will find out which investments are appropriate for each of the three pools of money you've identified.

THE RULES

Rule One: Every investment breaks down to either being a *lender* or being an *owner*.

The lender is going to have more security and usually a predictable income stream; the owner is going to have less security and more opportunity to be rewarded.

37

Rule Two: The higher the expected growth of the investment, the higher the risk.

The lower the risk, the lower the expected return.

Rule Three: Each investment carries with it a different level of risk.

If you are a lender (fixed income or bonds), there is little or no room for growth, and also less risk. If you're an owner (stock), there is a potential for growth, but there is also more risk. So your next question might be how do you measure that risk?

The standard measurements of risk are beta and volatility (standard deviation): Most institutions use beta to measure risk compared to the market. Beta is a measure of the risk of an investment compared to that of the market. This is a good way for institutions to measure risk; however, it is often not very useful for individuals since we don't look at risk in relative terms. The market is said to have a beta of 1.0. If a fund has a beta of 0.6, it is said to be 60 percent as risky as the market.

Don't let the term *volatility* be intimidating—it's simply investment jargon for frequency and amount of change. Volatility is a measure of total risk, instead of relative risk like beta. It can be statistically measured using *standard deviation*. Standard deviation describes how far from the average performance the monthly performance has been, either higher or lower. In investment circles, the word *mean* often is used instead of *average*. The standard deviation measurement helps explain what the distribution of returns will likely be. The greater the range of returns, the greater the risk. Generally, the current price of a security reflects the expected total return of its investment and its perceived risk.

When you bought your house, you took an unacknowledged risk. But you were willing to accept the risk because you were thinking long term. You weren't thinking, "What are housing prices going to do tomorrow?" You were investing over a 10- to 20-year time period, so you bought a home that you believed was a good value, one that met your needs, and that over the long term would be worth more than it was when you bought it. Consider how you would feel about the risk of owning a home if you looked at the market prices every day. It would be like, "The water main on Sixth Street broke; my house just dropped in value 10 percent." Odds are you wouldn't be a happy home owner if you monitored your home's market value every day.

Why are people more willing to accept risk when buying real estate? Because they don't purchase a house thinking that they might sell it tomorrow. They know that, despite occasional drops in the real estate market, their house is probably going to increase in value by the time they've paid off the mortgage in 15 or so years. The same is true for stocks held over long periods, but for some reason people don't think about stocks the way they think about real estate.

People use the term return *a lot in the stock market. Whenever you hear the word* return, *substitute the word* growth *in your mind. If you hear someone say the* return *on the stock market was 12.5 percent, say to yourself, the* growth *of the stock market was 12.5 percent.*

A general rule for risky investments: Every investment that is risky (stocks) will have twice the volatility of the expected return (see Exhibit 2-1).

If you invest for a short-term goal, you will probably want lower volatility and be willing to accept lower returns. If you invest for the long term, you can probably tolerate greater volatility in order to anticipate the potential for greater returns.

EXHIBIT 2-1 Risk Increases as Reward Increases

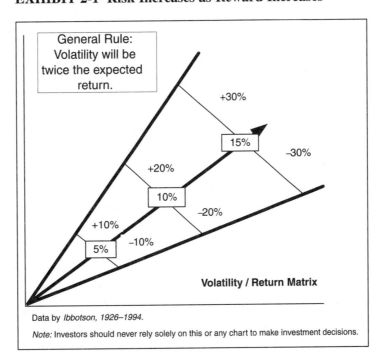

EXHIBIT 2-2 Asset Classes Perform Differently in Different Markets

There is no one asset class that is in favor all the time

Top Performing Markets	Years
S&P 500	1985, 1989, 1995, 1996, 1997, 1998
Small Stocks	1980, 1983, 1991, 1992
Foreign Stocks	1986, 1987, 1988, 1993, 1994, 1995, 1999
Long-Term Bonds	1982, 1984
Treasury Bills	1981, 1990

Source: Centurion Capital Management. Past performance is no guarantee of future results.

Rule Four: Different investments behave differently.

As an example, during the real estate boom of the 1970s, the stock market had some of its worst years. Large-cap stocks have been the top asset class in the last few years, and before that, internationals were the top class. As you can see from Exhibit 2-2, sometimes small stocks do better; sometimes large stocks do better; sometimes international stocks do better. In risky investments, it's very hard to predict which will do better at any given time.

The theoretical rule is you will have different returns for different investment classes.

Rule Five: Expect the unexpected.

When it comes to the stock market, you have to expect the unexpected. It's nearly impossible to guess what the market is going to do over any span of time. What we want you to do is try to mentally prepare for the average corrections. At times, the market has gone down and stayed down for a long time. At other times, it just dipped and flipped back up again. The 1990s were a time of sharp, quick drops and dramatic movements upward. This might be because the inflow of information is much faster, or it may just be due to economic conditions. Our inflation rate is down; we're balancing the budget; our political system is stable; and corporations are generating steady profits. All these factors combine to create a bull market.

EXHIBIT 2-3 Historical Frequency of Declines

Routine (−5%)	Moderate (−10%)	Severe (−15%)	Bear Market (−20% or Greater)
3 Times / Year	Once / Year	Once / 2 Years	Once / 3 Years

Source: Ned Davis Research
Note: Past performance does not guarantee future results.
Investors should not rely solely on this chart to make investment decisions.

- Since WWII, there have been 42 years with positive market returns and only 11 years with negative returns.
- The best return was 45 percent in 1954.
- The worst was −29.7 percent in 1974.
- The median was 16.5.
- The market has only gone down two years in a row once: 1973 and 1974.

The good times in the market have far outpaced the down periods, as you can see. When the economy is healthy and the market is on a roll, stock prices can rise for years. During the last 50 years, the stock market has seen four major bull markets, with moves over 100 percent. However, there were meaningful declines in between, even in those positive environments. So be prepared for substantial drops even in a good environment (see Exhibit 2-3), if you're investing in stocks.

THE SIX CONCEPTS

Your goal as a first time investor should be to find an investment strategy that delivers a consistent and specific result and one that can be duplicated. Most first time investors believe investing is nothing more than a matter of luck. They listen to investment tips and success stories. They chase the hot stock or attempt to time the market's performance. Both are strategies that are costly to implement, have an extremely low probability of success, and are ineffective in adding value. The problem is that occasional success stories can't be replicated. If they could, we'd be able to replicate the results of last year's best mutual fund.

Our desire is to have you focus on an overall investment strategy and portfolio, rather than to view a specific investment in isolation, since academic studies tell us that each investment should be evaluated for its contribution to a portfolio's total return.

Also, most first time investors have never heard the academic theories of investing. They get their information from the news media, magazines, or TV. This "information" consists mostly of day-to-day noise and confusing distractions. Most is misguided, sensational, and lacks any theoretical foundation. Many false ideas are so widespread that the public, for the most part, simply accepts them as fact.

To be successful you need to avoid the noise out there. When you listen to the nightly news, sit back and ask yourself, "What does this really have to do with me?" Worrying about the daily moves of the stock market is like watching another police car chase on the 6 o'clock news.

Instead of listening to misinformation as a strategy for investing, let's examine the six basic investment concepts that will give you the highest possible probability for success.

Checklist:

1. The importance of asset allocation
2. Understanding diversification
3. Combining dissimilar investments
4. Adding time to your investment program
5. The magic of compounding
6. Understanding asset-class investing

Did you know there are two types of diversification? You can diversify among different asset classes (asset allocation) and within asset classes.

Concept One: The Importance of Asset Allocation

Although asset allocation and diversification often are used interchangeably, don't confuse the two strategies. Asset allocation is the way you divide your money among the basic asset classes—stocks, bonds, and cash investments. You are only well-diversified if you allocate across different asset classes. Determining the right asset allocation is a big deal. It can be critical to your investment success.

Stocks have the highest average total return over the long run, but they are often the most volatile in the short run. Cash equivalents have the lowest return, but are the least volatile. Bond volatility falls in the middle. Even if stocks outperform the other asset classes over a period of years, they do not do so every year. Wise asset allocation helps you manage risk and maximize returns.

Allocating assets among all classes reduces your risk if one class significantly underperforms another.

Asset allocation is now widely understood by successful investors to be the single most important determinant of the long-term performance of any investment portfolio.

As illustrated in Exhibit 2-4, over 90 percent of a portfolio's total return variation is due to its asset allocation. The Brinson, Hood, and Beebower study found that asset allocation accounted for 91.5 percent of the total vari-

EXHIBIT 2-4 Explanation of Total Return Variation

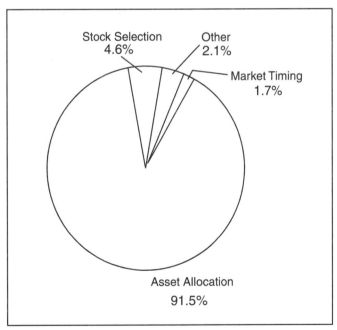

Source: Financial Analysts Journal, *G.P. Brinson,*
B.D. Singer, and G.L. Beebower
May–June 1991

ation in returns. That means that less than 7 percent of a fund's performance was due to the choice of individual stocks and bonds, market timing, security selection, transaction costs, and other miscellaneous items combined.

The goal of asset allocation is to combine investments in different asset classes to maximize the growth of your portfolio for each unit of risk you take.

 Suppose all your money is invested in stocks and you need to sell some of your holdings to meet an emergency. If the stocks in your mutual funds are depressed when you need to sell, you could be forced to take a loss on your investment. Owning other investments would give you flexibility in raising needed cash while allowing you to hold your stocks until prices improved. A diversified portfolio invested in several asset classes provides both liquidity and comparative stability.

You also diversify to protect yourself against the risk of outliving your money. Diversify into riskier assets like stocks, or you run the risk of seeing the value of your assets erode away as inflation and taxation take their toll.

Concept Two: Understanding Diversification

Diversification means not putting all your eggs in one basket. The first way to do that is to allocate your investments among asset classes as mentioned previously. The other is to spread your risk within an asset class.

In the financial world, diversification means not having all your money in any one type of investment. Mutual funds, by design, are often diversified within an asset class. A stock mutual fund typically has a lot of stocks in it. Investing in mutual funds, or a broad selection of investments within each asset class, is the first step you can take to reduce your investment risk. Your overall investment performance should be less volatile with a broad variety of investments rather than in a single type. Exhibit 2-5 illustrates the importance of diversification.

Graph 1 in Exhibit 2-5 illustrates a single investment of $10,000 at an 8 percent return during 25 years. Graph 2 in Exhibit 2-5 illustrates diversifying the same $10,000 investment into five separate $2,000 amounts, producing various returns. Three of the five investments showed a lower return than the single investment, but the total for the diversified portfolio was substantially higher. While it's true you would have been further ahead by being invested in just the "hot" stock, that's a matter of luck and not likely to be predictable beforehand.

EXHIBIT 2-5 The Importance of Diversification. These graphs illustrate the compounding growth on two $10,000 investments over a 25-year period. The $10,000 on the left assumes a single investment at an 8% return. The graph on the right assumes diversification of $10,000 into five $2,000 investments at different returns.

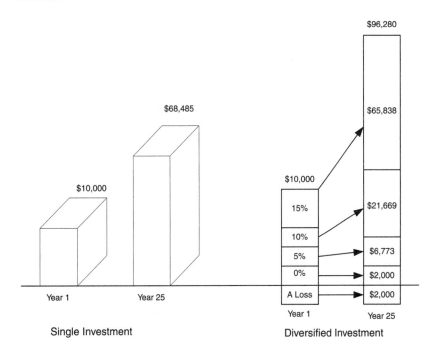

While three of the five investments were a lower return than the single investment, the total for the diversified side was substantially higher.

Each stock responds differently to changes in the economy and investment marketplace. The trick is to own a variety of assets because a short-term decline in one can be balanced by others that are stable or going up in value. For example, during the 1980s biotech stocks soared, and in the 1990s technology stocks boomed.

Effective and Ineffective Diversification. Diversification is a prudent method for managing certain types of investment risk. For example, unsystematic risks, those risks associated with individual securities, can be reduced through diversification. However, it doesn't work to invest all your assets in the same market segment, or in segments that tend to move in tandem. The risk is that all your investments could decrease in value at the same time. For instance, investing in the Standard and Poor's 500 stock index and the Dow Jones Industrial Average would be ineffective diversification since both tend to move in the same direction at the same time. Both are indexes composed of large capitalized companies in the United States.

Effective diversification is having a portfolio of investments that tend to move dissimilarly. The overall risk of a portfolio is *not* the average risk of each of the investments. In fact, you can have a low-risk portfolio that is actually made up of high-risk assets. When investments are combined in this way, you have achieved effective diversification.

Effective diversification reduces extreme price fluctuations and smooths out returns.

Concept Three: Combining Dissimilar Investments

Purchasing asset classes with a low correlation toward each other is the Nobel Prize–winning secret for achieving better portfolio consistency (Exhibit 2-6).

 What do we mean by low correlation? Technically, correlation (Exhibit 2-7) is a statistical measure of the degree to which the movement of two variables is related. A low correlation means that two assets are moving in different cycles, producing a negative cross-correlation.

EXHIBIT 2.6 Efficient Diversification Chart

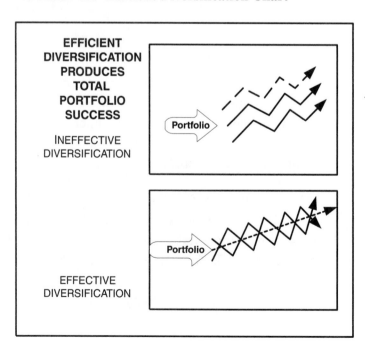

EXHIBIT 2-7 Correlation for Asset Classes

	Fixed Income			U.S. Stocks		International Stocks	
	Money Market	One Year Fixed	Five Year Fixed	Large Co.	Small Co.	Large Co.	Small Co.
Money Market	1.000						
One Year Fixed	0.913	1.000					
Five Year Fixed	0.486	0.735	1.000				
U.S. Large Company Stocks	–0.041	0.010	0.227	1.000			
U.S. Small Company Stocks	–0.085	–0.041	0.107	0.763	1.000		
Int'l Large Company Stocks	–0.218	–0.181	–0.077	0.487	0.442	1.000	
Int'l Small Company Stocks	–0.294	–0.369	–0.286	0.377	0.301	0.821	1.000

A high correlation means two assets move in tandem. A so-called *positive* covariance indicates that asset returns move together, where a *negative* covariance means they vary inversely. This kind of diversification reduces risk.

If portfolios of volatile stocks are put together in a similar way, the portfolio as a whole will actually be less risky than any one of the individual stocks in it. It is this negative covariance that plays the critical role in successful management of stock portfolios.

Concept Four: Adding Time to Your Investment Program

Given enough time, investments that might otherwise seem unattractive may become highly desirable. The longer the time period over which investments are held, the closer actual returns in a portfolio will come to the expected average. This means short-term market fluctuations will smooth out.

The real challenge is to commit to a discipline of long-term investing and to avoid compelling investment distractions. With a long-term view, you can better choose investments that have the best chances for success. By adding the essential ingredient of time to your investment plans, you can almost be assured of success.

Analysis shows that over and over again, the trade-off between risk and reward is driven by one key factor—time.

EXHIBIT 2-8 NASDAQ Composite (3/31/00–4/14/00)

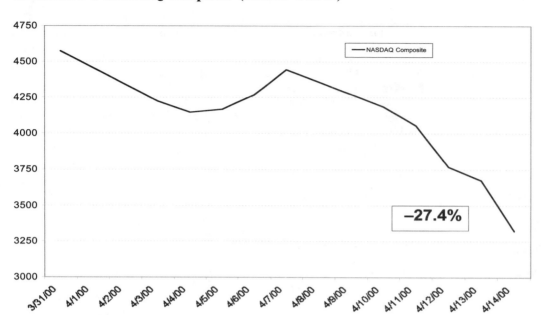

Source: Centurion Capital Management, 2000.

Exhibit 2-8 shows the NASDAQ for two weeks 3/31/00 through 4/14/00. The Composite was down 27 percent.

Exhibit 2-9 represents the NASDAQ from March 31, 2000 to June 30, 2000. It was down 13 percent over that short period.

The real story is in Exhibit 2-10. When you sit back and look at the year, the NASDAQ was up 47 percent. If you look at it from a more distant time, the drop isn't that big a deal. Time diminishes risk.

No sensible investor would invest in a stock for only one day, one month, or even one year. Such brief time periods are clearly too short for investment in stocks, because the expected variation in returns is too large in comparison to the average expected return. Such short-term holdings in stocks are not investments—they are speculations.

- If we measure an investment every three years, rather than every quarter, we can see satisfying progress that wouldn't be apparent on a quarterly measurement.

- In most cases, the time horizon that investors use as the standard to measure results is far too short, causing dissatisfaction with investment performance. This is perpetuated with information overload and a sense that you must do something with all the news you receive. Often doing less is better.

EXHIBIT 2-9 NASDAQ Composite (3/31/00–6/30/00)

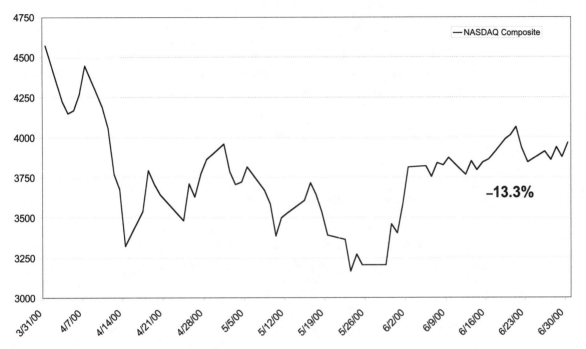

Source: Centurion Capital Management, 2000.

EXHIBIT 2-10 NASDAQ Composite (7/1/99–6/30/00)

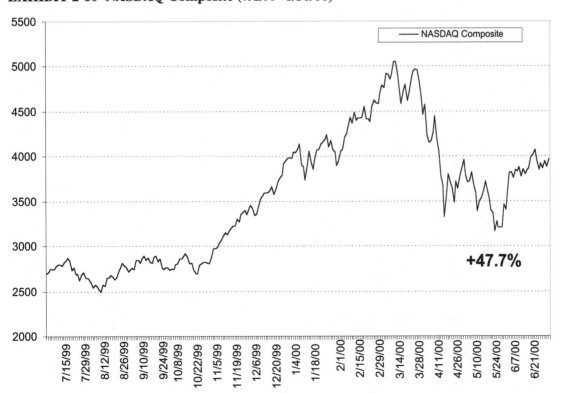

Source: Centurion Capital Management, 2000.

● Too often, people try to compress time. They have dreams that can only be reached by getting rich quick, but those attempts almost always end up on the losing side.

If you study Exhibit 2-11, you'll see that the investments made in any 1-year period could have gone up 54 percent or dropped 43 percent—but look what happens as you add time. The drops disappear. Look to any 20-year period and you will see that there are no down periods, only gains.

As you can see, equities become much less volatile the longer the period of time they're held.

Concept Five: The Magic of Compounding

Compounding means reinvesting the money you've made along with your principal. This means that over time dividends, interest, and capital gains grow exponentially. For example, a $100 investment earning compound inter-

EXHIBIT 2-11 Correlation of Risk Over Time

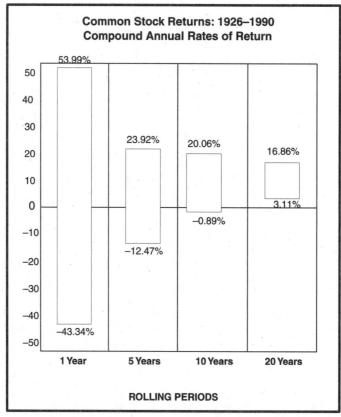

Source: Ibbotson Associates.

est at 10 percent a year would accumulate to $110 at the end of the first year and $121 at the end of the second year, and so on, based on the formula:

compound sum = (principal) (1 + interest rate) × (number of periods)

Let us show you what 12 percent can do over a six-year time frame. With an investment of $100,000 earning 12 percent every year, at the end of six years, you've got $200,000. Even 12 percent, over six years, can double your money. That's the magic of compounding. Basically, you get growth on any previous growth that you have had (Exhibit 2-12).

Dollar Cost Averaging. Dollar cost averaging (Exhibit 2-13) is also a factor of the compounding process. You can buy stocks or mutual funds at regular intervals with a fixed dollar amount. Under this system an investor buys by the dollar's worth rather than by the number of shares. When the price is down you are able to buy more shares, when the price is up you buy less. By adding shares over time you also get the compounding effect. It is important to note that taking money out systematically can be very disruptive in a volatile investment.

EXHIBIT 2-12 The Power of Compounding

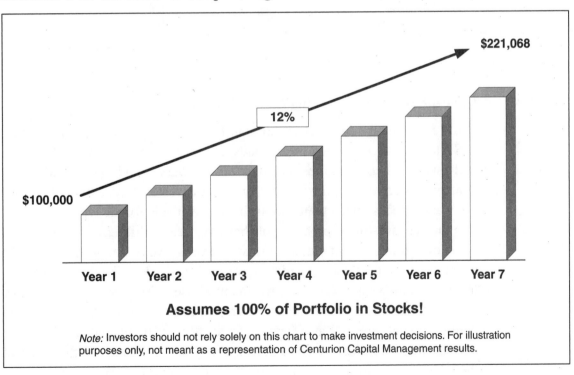

Assumes 100% of Portfolio in Stocks!

Note: Investors should not rely solely on this chart to make investment decisions. For illustration purposes only, not meant as a representation of Centurion Capital Management results.

EXHIBIT 2-13 Dollar Cost Averaging

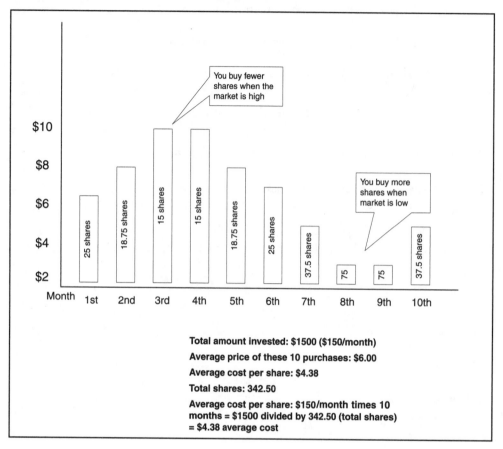

Concept Six: Understanding Asset-Class Investing

What Is an Asset Class? There are four basic asset classes you can invest in: U.S. stocks, international stocks, bonds, and cash. There are other assets like real estate and commodities, but they are not very liquid and are advanced strategies not really appropriate for first time investors to use by themselves. We want to focus on the major areas that are available for the typical investor.

In the investment process you have two clear differences: investment vehicles and investment classes, or asset classes. We're going to explain the different investment classes and then we're going to describe the ways (vehicles) you can use to buy these investment classes. Each asset class has specific risk characteristics and specific growth characteristics. Let's start with bonds or what you will also hear as fixed income. It's called fixed income because the income amount as a percentage is set, or "fixed," by the issuer of the bond. Bonds are yield-generating debt that you can own.

Look at Exhibit 2-14. The *x*-axis going from the bottom to the top shows maturity. Maturity is a measure that tells of the length the bond has until the debt is repaid. Typically the longer the maturity, the higher the risk.

The *y*-axis measures quality from left to right. Values further to the right represent lower quality. Typically the lower the quality, the higher the risk, and the higher the yield.

All fixed income investments fit somewhere in this box. In the lower left quadrant, you have short-term, high quality debt, for example: Treasury bills and CDs. In the upper left quadrant is long-term high quality bonds; for example, government or triple A rated bonds. In the upper right half is lower quality fixed income debt; at the bottom right is short-term lower quality debt such as commercial paper. Going up the *x*-axis are lower quality bonds more long-term in nature, like high-yield bonds. And you can be anywhere in between any of these boxes.

Equities, also called stocks, refer to owning a portion of a company. In Exhibit 2-15 the *x*-axis measures the size of companies from small to big; typically the smaller the company, the higher the risk. The *y*-axis left to right shows value to growth; typically the higher the growth, the higher the risk of the stocks (and the higher the expected rewards).

EXHIBIT 2-14 The Bond Asset Classes

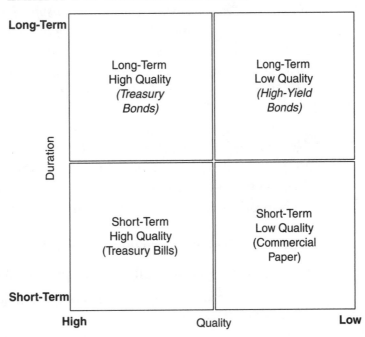

EXHIBIT 2-15 The Domestic Equities Asset Classes

Large-Cap Value	Large-Cap Growth
Small-Cap Value	Small-Cap Growth

Large-Cap

Size

Small-Cap

Value   Style   Growth

All U.S. stocks fit somewhere in this box. High growth companies are further to the right; more conservative companies to the left. For example, companies like eBay or Yahoo are growth companies because they grow aggressively, not necessarily generating as much earnings, and paying very few dividends because they're reinvesting all their money. Companies like Edison Utilities or Dupont are value companies because they pay a high dividend and are more of a conservative company so they are further to the left. All are quite large. The larger the company, the higher up the box it is.

With international equities, the scale is the same as with U.S. equities. The *y*-axis left-to-right shows value to growth. Again, as with U.S. equities, the higher the risk, the higher the return. You will find emerging market stocks in the growth area and most are small cap (Exhibit 2-16). The smaller the companies, the higher the risk, and so, too, the potential rewards.

Why Put Money in International Stocks?

1. Foreign stocks historically have outperformed U.S. stocks.

2. Foreign stocks provide good diversification due to their low correlation with U.S. markets.

EXHIBIT 2-16 The International Equities Asset Classes

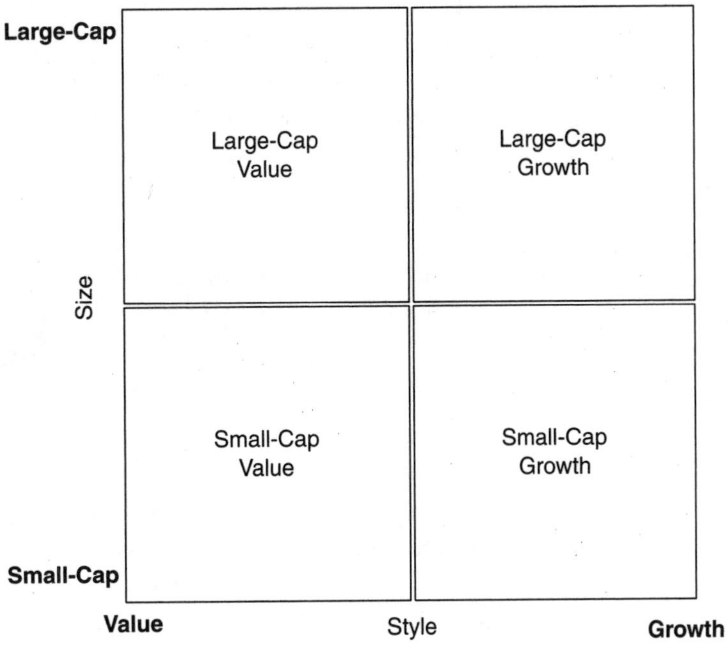

Large-Cap Value	Large-Cap Growth
Small-Cap Value	Small-Cap Growth

(Vertical axis: Size, from Large-Cap at top to Small-Cap at bottom. Horizontal axis: Style, from Value on left to Growth on right.)

While it is true that international stocks measured by Morgan Stanley Capital International's EAFE Index have at times outperformed the S&P 500 since 1970, this occurs often because foreign currencies have outperformed the U.S. dollar. Instead of investing in international equities for higher returns, you should include them in your portfolio to reduce risk. The international and U.S. equity markets historically have had low correlation; they do not tend to move together.

The world is getting smaller, and that's true for the world's stock markets too. The correlation across countries has been on the rise for many years, especially when the United States has a substantial fall. Be aware that diversifying across countries doesn't provide the protection it once did.

Given the data, you might want to own fixed income investments to provide stability to your portfolio, not to generate high returns. High returns would come from equities. Fixed income securities can help offset the risk of your equity holdings and, therefore, lower the risk of your overall portfolio. You can best do this by using short-term fixed income securities rather than long-term bonds. Short-term bonds have less volatility and a lower correla-

tion with stocks and are a better choice for your portfolio. They will allow you to invest a larger percentage of your money in stocks while maintaining low portfolio risk.

Equities typically have high risk, high return, and the time horizon should be longer. Bonds and money market funds are lower risk, lower return, with a shorter time horizon.

Results for Various Asset Classes. As you can see, over the last 30 years these investments have all done quite well. But please remember that in any given 1-, 3- or 5-year period the results would look quite different to this 30-year snapshot.

Exhibit 2-17 shows the rate of return for the last 30 years for each of the asset classes; the beta; the averages of the worst four quarters and the worst four years.

As we go through each asset class you will see a riskometer (see Exhibit 2-18). The further to the right the riskometer needle, the more risky the investment and the higher the potential rewards. For simplification purposes we are using a five point scale. Time and your risk profile are the biggest drivers determining which asset classes you will choose for each of the three money drills in your IPS. The growth rate percentages shown in Exhibit 2-18 are a rough estimation of the types of gains you should be targeting in each of the risk areas over time.

EXHIBIT 2-17 Individual Asset Classes

	Rate of Return Over 30 Yrs	Beta	Average of Worst Four Quarters	Average of Worst Four Years
Large-Cap Growth	12.9	1.13	−29.7	−29.7
Large-Cap Value	15.6	0.83	−17.6	−10.9
Small-Cap Growth	8.9	1.4	−29.5	−28.8
Small-Cap Value	17.6	1.1	−23.2	−18.4
EAFE	13.2	0.75	−19.5	−17.8
Long-Term Gov. Bonds	8.9	0.25	−10.3	−5.8
Short-Term Gov. Bonds	7.7	0.0	−0.4	3.8

Source: Ibbotson and Associates

EXHIBIT 2-18 Riskometer Scale

Level of Decline (%)	Target Growth Rate (%)	Approximate Time Frame	Riskometer
3	3–5	0–6 months	RISKOMETER
6	5–6	3–12 months	RISKOMETER
8	6–8	6 mos.–2 yrs.	RISKOMETER
10	8–9	18 mos.–3 yrs.	RISKOMETER
15	9–11	3–5 years	RISKOMETER
23	10–13	5–7 years	RISKOMETER
35	11–14	5–10 years	RISKOMETER
50	12–15	5–10 years	RISKOMETER

HOW TO INVEST IN THESE ASSET CLASSES

There are several ways to invest in the asset classes we have just covered. Which investment vehicle will you choose to invest in these asset classes? It depends on your constraints: the amount of money you have, your time horizon, your need for liquidity, your tax situation, and the legal structure, along with your unique circumstances.

Using the weight-loss analogy, two classes for losing weight are exercise and dieting. If you decide to exercise, you could choose as your vehicle kickboxing, aerobics, running, and so on. Each weight-loss vehicle has different constraints. For example, if you have bad knees, you shouldn't be kickboxing.

You're going to get a different end-result depending on the vehicle you use. Examples of vehicles you might choose for getting invested in stocks are buying individual stocks, buying mutual funds, or through variable annuities. You need to determine which of the different investment vehicles will provide the most desirable returns for *you*, to meet *your* goals.

 Each investment vehicle also has different constraints, which we covered in Section One. The constraints, for example, tax considerations, are on the vehicles you choose to buy those asset classes. If you buy stock directly, you only pay taxes on dividends while you own it and capital gains when you sell it (hopefully, long term in nature). If you buy stock through a mutual fund, tax issues are out of your control. The mutual fund manager decides how much he or she will realize in taxes in any given year. If you buy stock through a variable annuity, there are no tax constraints until you get your cash out, and then it is taxed at income level, not the capital gains rate. So the risk and return for the stocks is the same, but the constraints are determined by the investment vehicle you use to buy the asset class.

A mutual fund is an investment company that makes investments on behalf of its participants who share common financial goals.

UNDERSTANDING THE VEHICLES—MUTUAL FUNDS

Advantages	*Disadvantages*
Low minimum investment	*No tax control*
Diversification	*No investment control*
Liquidity	*No customized investing*
Professional Management	

We're not going to get into analyzing which of the hundreds of mutual funds you should buy—there are so many and that really is a job for a professional. What you need to know when working with an advisor or a financial planner, or doing it yourself, is whether the recommendations fit you or not. The first step toward that end is understanding how things work.

Mutual funds continually issue new shares of the fund for sale to the public. The number of shares and the price are directly related to the value of the securities the mutual fund holds. A fund's share price can change from day to day, depending on the daily value of its underlying securities.

Think of a mutual fund as a financial intermediary that pools all its investors' funds together and buys stocks, bonds, or other assets on behalf of the group as a whole. Each investor receives a certificate of ownership and a regular statement of his or her account indicating the value of the shares of the total investment pool.

 A stock mutual fund is called an equity fund, which is usually a higher growth vehicle. Over the last 15 years, the average stock mutual fund has captured about 13.3 percent growth. But remember the rule: The volatility will be twice the expected return. Obviously, an equity mutual fund is not an appropriate investment for your short-term money. Nor is it a good place for your intermediate money. But the time frame for your long-term money is five years or more, so an equity mutual fund is a good choice.

Exhibit 2-19 shows the ranking of the top 20 mutual funds that had 200 percent returns in 1999. Late in 2000 more than half had negative returns.

EXHIBIT 2-19 Top 20 Mutual Funds of 1999 Burn Investors. These 20 funds had returns over 200 percent in 1999. Ah, but where are they today? Answer: Over half show negative returns. Here's a handy table to remind you that chasing returns isn't always the best way to invest.

Fund Name	Investment Category	Annual Ret.— 1999	Total Ret.— 1 Mo.	Total Ret.— 3 Mo.	Total Ret.— YTD
Nicholas-Apple GlbTech I	Specialty-Tech	493.73	(5.54)	1.11	3.45
Warburg Pincus Adv Japan Sm	Japan Stock	329.68	(18.41)	(28.85)	(53.53)
MAS Small Cap Growth Instl	Growth	313.91	(7.87)	(2.73)	(4.10)
Van Wagoner Emerging Growth	Growth	291.15	3.40	29.61	21.90
Nevis Fund	Growth	286.53	(10.53)	(2.07)	3.05
Monument Internet A	Specialty-Tech	273.15	(5.56)	(5.71)	(25.89)
Driehaus Asia Pacific Growth	Pac./Asia Stock	264.49	(9.36)	(14.31)	(23.02)
Warburg Pincus Adv Japan Growth	Japan Stock	260.27	(17.52)	(31.18)	(52.40)
Amerindo Technology D	Specialty-Tech	248.86	(7.33)	(6.71)	(32.56)
PBHG Technology & Commun	Specialty-Tech	243.89	(8.85)	4.09	6.22
Fidelity Japan Smaller Co	Japan Stock	237.42	(16.51)	(20.16)	(36.05)
Van Wagoner Post-Venture	Growth	237.22	2.07	24.54	7.72
ProFunds UltraOTC Inv	Growth	233.26	(10.19)	(17.27)	(25.90)
Van Wagoner Technology	Specialty-Tech	223.76	2.57	23.46	12.78
BlackRock Micro-Cap Eq Inst	Growth	221.54	(14.61)	(1.68)	8.42
Kinetics Internet	Specialty-Tech	216.44	(2.82)	(11.07)	(30.03)
Warburg Pincus Intl Sm Comm	Foreign Stock	216.42	(6.55)	(9.06)	(7.16)
Driehaus International Disc	Foreign Stock	213.65	(4.62)	(6.50)	4.46
Thurlow Growth	Growth	213.21	(15.35)	(19.94)	(29.87)
Firsthand Technology Innovat	Specialty-Tech	212.34	(12.17)	(4.04)	10.80

Analyzing funds is not a part-time effort so if you decide to do it for yourself, look for good, long-term track records, not last year's top performance. Don't worry too much about picking the wrong funds, since most funds do as well as their underlying asset classes.

The main reasons people invest in mutual funds are convenience, accessing professional knowledge, and the opportunity to earn higher returns through a combination of growth and reinvestment of dividends. To understand why mutual funds are so popular, let's examine just how mutual funds work.

How Mutual Funds Work

The manager of the mutual fund uses the pool of capital to buy a variety of individual stocks, bonds, or money market instruments based on the advertised financial objectives of the fund. These objectives cover a wide range. Some funds follow aggressive policies, involving greater risk in search of higher returns. Others seek current income and no risk. Since each mutual fund has a specific investment objective, the investor has the ability to select a variety of funds to meet asset allocation and diversification needs.

When you purchase mutual fund shares, you own them at *net asset value*. This is the value of the fund's total investment, minus any debt, divided by the number of outstanding shares. For example, if the fund's investment value is $26,000,000 with no debt and 1,000,000 shares outstanding: the net asset value (NAV) would be $26 per share. The NAV is not a fixed figure because it must reflect the daily change in the price of the securities within the fund's portfolio.

In a regular mutual fund that includes thousands and often millions of shares, the NAV is calculated on a daily basis without commissions, in full and fractional units, with values moving up or down along with the stock and bond markets.

 The biggest mistake that most investors make when buying mutual funds is looking first (and sometimes only) at the prior performance of the fund. That's like looking toward the East for the sunset.

There are two basic kinds of costs:

1. Management fees
2. Sales charges

Management Fees. Because of the large amounts of assets under management, investment companies are able to offer *economies of scale,* or competitive fee schedules, to their customers. Fund costs are an equally important factor in the return that you earn from a mutual fund. Fees are deducted from your investment. All other things being equal, high fees and other charges depress your returns.

The management fees charged depend on the complexity of the asset management demands. Foreign equity management requires substantially more research, specialized implementation, and higher transaction costs than the management of a U.S. government bond fund. Asset management fees reflect those differences. Equity mutual fund fees are higher than bond mutual fund fees.

Actively managed funds typically have higher fees than index funds since they seek to outperform the indexes and must, therefore, invest substantially in research and are typically more active in trading.

Fee comparisons are particularly important (see Exhibit 2-20). Remember to compare the proverbial apples to apples—in this case, similar equities to equity mutual funds; and similar bonds to bond mutual funds.

Don't concentrate on fees as much as you concentrate on after fee performance. While everyone talks about fees, it's far more important that managers earn their fees, than that they charge very little. This is obviously not so in an index fund where cost should be the only difference among the funds.

EXHIBIT 2-20 Fee Comparisons of Various Mutual Funds

Mutual Fund	Annual Performance (%)	Management Fees (%)	Net Performance (%)
Foreign Equities	12.50	1.25	11.25
U.S. Large-Cap	12.50	1.00	11.50
U.S. Small-Cap	13.00	1.20	11.8
Investment-Grade Bonds	7.80	0.65	7.15
High-Yield Bonds	9.25	0.75	8.50
Foreign Bonds	9.25	0.90	8.35

Sales Charges. Sales charges, or loads, are commissions paid on the sale of mutual funds. In the past, all commissions were simply charged up front, but that has changed. There are now several ways mutual fund companies charge fees.

The sales charge is subtracted from the initial mutual fund investment. A no-load fund does not have this charge, although other fees or service charges may be buried in its cost structure. Don't be misled: Nearly all mutual funds have a sales charge. Some are hidden—some are not. Let's talk about the ones that you can see.

A *front-end* load mutual fund charges a fee when an investor buys it. Loaded mutual funds can also be *back-end* load—having a deferred sales charge—and are sometimes known as *B-shares.* This option has higher internal costs. If you decide to redeem your shares early, usually within the first five years, you pay a surrender charge.

A customer who redeems shares in the first year of ownership would typically pay a five percent sales charge. The amount would drop by an equal amount each year. After six years, the shares could be redeemed without further charge.

- A-shares charge the commission all at once.
- B-shares have a contingent deferred sales charge. They are more popular with brokers because you don't pay any up-front load, but every year they take out the equivalent of 1 percent.
- C shares typically have even higher internal expenses and pay the selling broker up to 1 percent per year based on the amount of the assets. This fee comes directly from your investment performance. C-shares may have no up-front fee, but a possible 1 percent deferred sales charge in the first year (sometimes longer), and higher annual expenses (up to 1 percent extra per year).

No-load mutual funds do *not* mean *no cost.* Some no-load funds charge a redemption fee of 1 to 2 percent of the net asset value of the shares to cover expenses mainly incurred by advertising. Buying a no-load mutual fund is like doing your own plumbing work. You can save money if you know what you're doing; but if you don't have the required time and expertise, you can make a serious mistake. We highly recommend working with an investment advisor who can offer the same no-load funds. Another important point to consider is that when you call a mutual fund company with a question, you are serviced by an employee of the mutual fund company, and the advice you receive may be biased. Remember, someone had to pay for the ads in the magazines.

Investors who are truly devoted to learning about financial matters, and who follow financial news and read enough to keep themselves well informed, may be able to do this for themselves. Most investors are not in this category and are well advised to seek professional guidance for their investments.

UNDERSTANDING YOUR INSTRUCTION MANUAL—THE PROSPECTUS

A survey by the Investment Company Institute, the mutual fund industry's trade group, discovered that only half of the fund shareholders consult a prospectus before investing. A jargon-filled mutual fund prospectus may not be enthralling, but it's a must-read for would-be first time investors. It describes investment objectives, strategies, and risks, and is required by the federal government as a protection for investors. Any misstatements or omissions can lead to stiff penalties; thus, the tendency for legalese.

You can start by identifying the type of asset class mutual fund you are interested in and request a prospectus by calling or writing the fund, or asking a broker or financial planner. When you get it, check the date to make sure it is current—such documents must be updated at least once a year.

Here's what to look for in a mutual fund prospectus:

Minimums. If the minimum amount required to open an account is too high for you, read no further.

Investment Objective. At the core of the prospectus is a description of the fund's investments and the portfolio manager's philosophy. The objective should outline what types of securities the fund buys and the policies regarding the quality of those investments. If the fund has more than 25 percent of its assets in one industry or holds bonds rated below investment quality, these policies must be included in the prospectus.

A global equity fund, for example, earns a high level of total return through investments in world capital markets. A typical balanced fund strives to obtain income equally with capital growth, while the investment objective of a long-term municipal bond fund is to preserve capital by seeking a high level of interest income exempt from federal income tax.

Performance. This bottom-line information on how funds have fared over the last decade shows you what you would have earned in per-share dividends and capital gains distributions, and any increase or decrease in the value of that share during the year. The portfolio turnover rate reveals how actively the fund trades securities. The higher the turnover, the greater the fund's brokerage costs.

Risk. Different investors can tolerate various risk levels. In this section of the prospectus, the fund should describe the potential for risk. For instance, a fund that invests in only one portion of the economy may offer greater risk than a highly diversified fund, while a fund that invests in well-established companies may be less risky than one that favors start-up companies.

Other risks are associated with certain types of funds or securities. Bond funds are susceptible to interest rate changes, while fixed income savings and investment vehicles are subject to inflation risks.

Fees. Management and accounting fees and the cost of printing and mailing reports to shareholders are internal charges that should be evaluated. Generally, a company that keeps its expenses—excluding sales fees—at 1 percent or less of its assets is considered a low-cost fund. A fund with expenses above 1.5 percent of its assets is viewed as high-cost.

Fees are required to be summarized in a table in the front of the prospectus. Other charges to consider are minimum fees for subsequent investments or fees for switching from one fund to another in the same family.

Management. When you're putting money in a mutual fund, you're paying for professional management. Consider the fund's managers to evaluate investment philosophy (how they manage the money using various asset classes), and to find out whether the portfolio is managed by an individual or committee.

Services. This section tells you if features such as check-writing or automatic investing are available.

Buying or Selling Shares. Information in this section details how to get in and out of a fund and whether there's a charge for redeeming shares.

Additional Information. Other information, such as securities in the fund's portfolio at the end of its fiscal year, is included in a Statement of Additional Information, also called Part B of the prospectus. Funds must provide this information free on request.

Other tools to evaluate mutual funds include news accounts and the fund's annual report. Make sure you are comparing apples to apples. Magazines measure funds during different time periods and use different criteria, which could affect a fund's ranking.

With more than the estimated six thousand mutual funds to choose from, many investors feel overwhelmed when comparing possible investments, particularly when they have to wade through prospectuses that make no sense.

The good news is that a movement is afoot to simplify the language used in prospectuses. The Securities and Exchange Commission (SEC) is recommending the creation of a clearly written one-page summary to accompany these documents.

The SEC also is demanding use of plain English. The new rules are going to target the fund booklets. Hopefully, by the time you read this book, the SEC and the mutual fund companies will have adopted their new language called "plain English." The SEC has adopted rules that will force mutual funds to ditch the legalese and translate their prospectuses—which most people toss in the trash unread—into easily understood language. The SEC is going to coach prospectus writers on how to translate common financial world jargon, how to write in the active voice, and how to find a strong verb that lies hidden in the text.

Also, fund companies may distribute a streamlined profile that includes a mutual fund's vital statistics. This is a victory for the consumer, at least for those who care enough to follow through and do their homework. Both documents will contain a 10-year bar chart of fund performance—a table comparing its performance to the market index and a description of the risk involved in the investment. A three-to-six-page profile also will summarize the fund's fees, risks, and investment objectives at the beginning of the document.

Now, for you Internet investors whose printers have choked trying to download a 20-page prospectus, this should be a relief. You will be able to make side-by-side comparisons of different funds. Information will be more visible in a shorter document available online.

OTHER THINGS YOU SHOULD KNOW ABOUT MUTUAL FUNDS

Dividends

Dividends and capital gains (the profits from a sale of stock) are paid in proportion to the number of mutual fund shares you own. So even if you invest a few hundred dollars, you get the same investment return per dollar as those who invest millions. The problem is you will have to pay taxes on this amount even if it is reinvested. You can use a variable annuity to defer those taxes until you plan to spend the money.

Statements

Any mutual fund in which you participate sends you a year-end statement itemizing the income you've received. You should save this sheet, along with other records of dividends, tax-exempt interest, and capital gains distributions, as well as records of the amounts received from the sale of shares for tax purposes.

Full-Time Professionals

When you invest in a mutual fund, you are hiring a team of professional investment managers to make complex investment judgments and handle complicated trading, record keeping, and safekeeping responsibilities for you.

Their job is to sift through the thousands of available investments in order to choose those that, in their judgment, are best suited to achieving the asset class investment goals of a fund as spelled out in the fund's prospectus.

Diversification in the Fund

Diversification is one important characteristic that attracts many investors to mutual funds. By owning a diverse portfolio of many stocks and/or bonds, investors can reduce the risk associated with owning any individual security.

A mutual fund is typically invested in 25 to 100 or more securities. Proper diversification ensures that the fund receives the highest possible return at the lowest possible risk given the objectives of the fund.

Mutual funds do not escape share price declines during major market downturns. For example, mutual funds that invested in stocks certainly declined during the October 27, 1997, market crash when the Dow Jones plunged 554.26 points. However, the unluckiest investors that month were individuals who had all of their money riding in Asian mutual funds. Some fund shares plunged in price by as much as 30 to 40 percent that month. Widely diversified mutual funds were impacted the least.

Low Initial Investment

Each mutual fund establishes the minimum amount required to make an initial investment, and then how much additional is required when investors want to add more. A majority of mutual funds have low initial minimums, some less than $1,000.

Liquidity

One of the key advantages of mutual funds stems from the liquidity provided by this investment. You can sell your shares at any time, and mutual funds have a ready market for their shares. Additionally, shareholders directly receive any dividend or interest payments earned by the fund. Payments are usually made on a quarterly basis. When the fund manager sells some of the investments at a profit, the net gain also is distributed, but net losses are retained by the fund. Inside the mutual fund, when the dividends or capital gains are disbursed, the NAV is reduced by the disbursement.

Audited Performance

All mutual funds are required to disclose historical data about the fund through their prospectuses—returns earned by the funds, operating expenses and other fees, and the funds' rate of trading turnover. The SEC audits these disclosures. Having the SEC on your side is like having a vigilant guard dog focused on the guy who's responsible for your money. Remember, all mutual funds are registered investments. This does not mean that the SEC recommends them, but it does mean they have reviewed them for abuse and fraud.

Automatic Reinvestment

One of the major benefits of mutual funds is that dividends can be reinvested automatically and converted into more shares (compounding effect).

Switching

Switching, or an exchange privilege, is offered by most mutual funds through so-called family or umbrella plans. Switching from one mutual fund to another accommodates changes in investment goals, as well as changes in the market and the economy. Outside of a retirement plan or variable annuity, this switching between mutual funds creates tax implications. For example, if you redeem a Franklin Growth and Income Fund and buy a Franklin NY Municipal Bond Fund, you have to pay taxes on the gains you earned.

 A reason to invest inside retirement plans and variable annuities is turnover.

Turnover

We've seen turnover in mutual funds go from around 10 to 12 percent 15 years ago to 90 percent today. This is the actual turnover of securities. Mutual funds have gotten so competitive, how does a portfolio manager get paid more bonus money this year than last year? The manager reaches for every last basis point of return—which is fine in a tax-free environment. Turnover is increased. If a manager is tax-sensitive, he or she has large unrealized capital gains built up in these funds. So if you're buying a fund now and you are taxable, you're buying into a tax liability—that's something to consider.

HOW DO THE VARIOUS MUTUAL FUND PARTIES WORK TOGETHER?

After you have written your check to the mutual fund, the mutual fund company sends that check on your behalf to an organization functioning as a transfer agent. Here your investment is recorded and processed and the safeguards come into play. Exhibit 2-21 shows how the parties involved interact. The agent transfers the money, not to the mutual fund's portfolio manager (the individual or firm that makes the investment decisions, technically known as the *investment advisor*), but to a custodian bank.

Once the custodian bank receives the money, it notifies the mutual fund that new money is available for investment. The fund manager checks a daily account balance sheet and "new monies" are invested according to the mutual fund's investment policy.

The Investment Company Act of 1940's requirement of independent custody of each mutual fund's assets has turned out to be the key provision that has sheltered the industry from potential trouble for half a century. Separate custody means a mutual fund's parent company can go belly-up without any loss to the fund's shareholders, because their assets are held apart from other funds and apart from the parent fund.

EXHIBIT 2-21 Relationship of Various Parties to a Mutual Fund

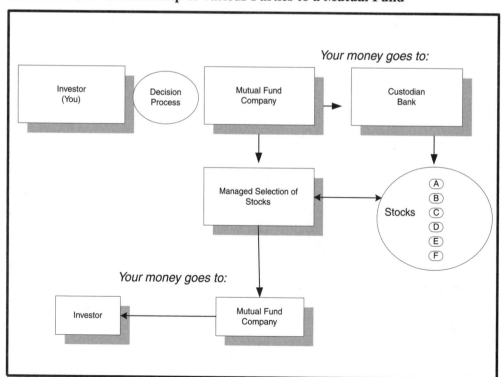

Contrast this business structure with the far less restrictive set-up between individual investors and a real estate promoter, for example; or investors and a stockbroker who may have direct access to clients' accounts. In any number of notorious incidents, individuals in such a position have taken the money and run.

The limited partnerships of the 1970s and 1980s were an excellent example of a poor business structure. During those years, many unregulated and unregistered limited partnerships were formed and investors sent their money directly to the limited partnership company. An unscrupulous promoter could simply write himself a check. Financial scandals were numerous.

The money manager of a mutual fund has no direct access to investors' cash.

The fund manager can only decide how to invest shareholders' money. The custodian who controls the underlying securities allows them to be traded or exchanged with other institutional investors only after getting proper documentation from the fund manager. The upshot of independent custody is that it's very difficult for a fund manager to use the money for his or her own purposes.

MAJOR TYPES OF MUTUAL FUNDS

Many fund management companies offer a number of different types of funds under one roof, often referred to as a *family of funds*. A family of funds might include a growth stock fund, an aggressive growth stock fund, a fund that invests in stocks and bonds, a tax-exempt bond fund, a money market fund, and perhaps many others. Most mutual funds permit their customers to exchange from one fund to another within the group for a small fee if their customers' personal investment objectives change.

Despite endless variations, there are basically three broad categories of mutual funds: those aimed at providing immediate income, those oriented toward long-term growth or appreciation, and those that stress tax-free returns. The fund's objectives will be stated at the opening of the prospectus, indicating whether the fund emphasizes high or low risk, stability, or speculation.

Funds generally fall into one of the following asset-class subcategories: stock, balanced, income, fixed income, cash, money market fund, tax-free, and specialized. Here it can get confusing. The terms most funds use are elementary descriptions of the actions of various types of asset classes. For instance, U.S. large or U.S. small would be simply called growth.

Index Funds

Think of these funds as whole baskets of stocks, representing the various stock market indexes. The S&P 500 index fund is by far the most common index fund for both institutional and individual investors. It tracks the performance of the Standard & Poor's 500 Index, a capitalization-weighted index of 500 large U.S. stocks. It is estimated that over 95 percent of all retail indexed monies are invested in S&P 500 index funds.

If you bought the Vanguard S&P 500 fund back in 1995, you would be up over 24 percent annually. And with no investing decisions to make, you would have had much more time to work on your golf game. Not bad! But index funds have their drawbacks.

For instance, there is absolutely no risk management. The index fund manager's mandate is to buy the same stocks that are in the S&P 500 index and weight them accordingly. If you like the S&P 500, you better like Microsoft, because in 2000 it represented 5 percent of the index. In fact, 30 percent of the S&P 500 is based on technology stocks. There are no increasing cash levels when valuations are high and the market looks lofty.

 Indexes are very important as a tool to compare your investments. We use them as a benchmark to ensure that the results of your underlying investments are appropriate and the manager is adding value. The easiest place to find these indexes is in newspapers or on the Internet.

U.S. Equities. You need indexes to compare properly. An index that measures large-cap value is called the Russell 1000 Value Index. If that is hard to find, the Dow Jones Industrial Average Index is close enough.

For large-cap growth, there is the Russell 1000 Growth Index. The NASDAQ composite is a good enough measure. If you want to just look at large-cap companies in general, the S&P 500 is a good measure that blends both growth and value.

If you want to compare small caps, you can look at the Russell 2000 Value or the Russell 2000 Growth. If you want to look at a blend of the two, the Russell 2000 does this.

In order to compare the results of your large-cap value mutual fund, compare it to its appropriate benchmark. And the appropriate benchmark here is the Russell 1000 Value, or the Dow Jones. It's not the S&P 500 because it includes growth stocks. Comparison for large-cap growth is the Russell 1000 Growth Index or the NASDAQ Composite, not the Dow Jones.

For international stocks, the Morgan Stanley EAFE Index is appropriate.

For bonds, the Shearson Lehman Aggregate Bond Index is appropriate.

Stock Funds

Stock funds emphasize growth. Dividend payouts typically are low. Most of these funds stress capital appreciation rather than immediate income.

Growth. Growth typically is defined as exceeding the growth of the economy. Investors look for companies and industries with a strong growth trend in sales and earnings. Growth companies typically sell at high price/earnings (P/E) ratios, reflecting the expectation that their growth will continue and "catch up" with the high valuations.

 Large-Cap Growth—An investment strategy that invests in stocks of large growth companies with an average capitalization of approximately $5 billion or greater.

 Mid-Cap Growth—An investment strategy that invests in stocks of mid-sized growth companies with an average capitalization of between $1 billion and $5 billion.

 Small-Cap Growth—An investment strategy that invests in stocks of smaller growth companies with an average capitalization of less than $1 billion.

Value. Value investors look for bargains. Value stocks have low book-to-market ratios, which means the stock is trading at a low price compared to its book value. Book value is defined as the company's assets on a balance sheet, less its liabilities. Book value is often figured on a per-share basis. If a company has a book value of $15 per share and the stock trades at $12, it may be perceived as a bargain.

The value manager tries to buy stocks at a perceived discount.

 Large-Cap Value—An investment strategy that invests in stocks of large value companies with an average capitalization of approximately $5 billion or greater.

 Mid-Cap Value—An investment strategy that invests in stocks of mid-sized value companies with an average capitalization of between $1 billion and $5 billion.

 Small-Cap Value—An investment strategy that invests in stocks of smaller value companies with an average capitalization of less than $1 billion.

Value and growth stocks tend to behave differently. There are market cycles when value stocks outperform growth stocks, and other periods when growth stocks outperform value stocks. In general, a growth investor's returns are more volatile than a value investor's returns. Both styles in a portfolio can even out performance over time. When one group is underperforming the market, the other is outperforming it.

International Equities. Read the prospectus to determine whether the fund tries to protect against moves in the dollar or not. Currency moves can have a significant effect on funds that do not hedge against currency fluctuations.

Diversified International—Focuses on large-cap stocks, typically leaving control in the hands of the manager, and they shift investments across countries and underlying stocks.

Diversified Emerging Market—Focus their investments on those economies that are still developing and growing. These are some of the most volatile funds.

International Growth—Focus their portfolios on stocks of high growth international companies.

International Value—Focus their portfolios on stocks of undervalued companies worldwide.

Balanced Funds

A balanced mutual fund includes two or more asset classes other than cash. In a typical balanced mutual fund, the asset classes are equities and fixed income securities.

These portfolios stress three main goals: income, capital appreciation, and preservation of capital. This type of fund balances holdings such as bonds, convertible securities, and preferred as well as common stock. The mix varies depending on the managers' views of the economy and market conditions.

The theory is that managers have a better crystal ball than you have at home, since they sit in front of a computer terminal all day looking at data. A balanced fund typically keeps 60 percent in stock and 40 percent in bonds. Since they are diversified into both bond and stock markets, these funds are most appropriate for investors who can only afford one fund.

Fixed Income Funds

The advertised investment objectives of fixed income funds are safety and income, rather than capital appreciation. Income funds invest in corporate bonds or government bonds; if they own any stocks at all, these are usually preferred shares. The danger is chasing higher yields and not looking at the risks.

U.S. Fixed Income. These are funds that invest in U.S. government and corporate bonds. They typically invest in higher quality investments with little risk of default.

High Yield. These funds typically invest in low quality debt and are subject to high risk of default. Therefore, they tend to offer a higher yield, but you increase your risk significantly.

Government. These are funds that invest in debt from the U.S. government. They are by their nature quite conservative, depending on the maturity of the underlying bonds.

International Fixed Income. These are funds that specialize in investing in bonds of international governments and are usually riskier than U.S. investments since they also suffer from currency shifts.

Global Bond Funds. These funds invest in foreign and U.S. bonds. Historically, global bond funds have outperformed domestic bond funds, but you assume additional risk.

Municipal Bond Funds. Municipal bond funds are nothing more than a large grouping of various municipal bonds. They may be appropriate when you are in high federal (28 percent and up) and state (5 percent or higher) tax brackets. Most municipal bond funds invest in municipal bonds of similar maturity (the number of years before the borrower, in this case the municipality, must pay back the money to you, the lender).

The key advantage of a bond fund is management. Unlike individual issues, the fund managers can switch bonds from time to time within a fund. A bond fund is always replacing bonds in its portfolio to maintain its average maturity objective.

Money Market Funds. Money market funds are the safest type of mutual fund if you are worried about the risk of losing your principal. Money market funds are like bank savings accounts in that the value of your investment does not fluctuate. This type of fund could be used as your core saving strategy.

Sector Funds. Sector funds, or specialty funds, tend to invest in stocks in specific industries. Sector funds should be avoided as large percentages of a portfolio. Investing in stocks of a single industry defeats a major purpose of investing in mutual funds—you give up the benefits of diversification. A sector fund would be something like the India Fund or a gold fund. They can be used to build a portfolio, but only in small amounts. We would caution anyone against placing a large percentage of a portfolio in these types of funds. The four largest sector funds are:

- Real estate funds
- Utilities funds
- Gold funds
- Technology funds

We've listed some of the main sectors that are available. There are, of course, many more specific sector funds, but these are the broadest sectors.

What types of funds are you most interested in? _____

_____

NOTES: _____

_____

_____

_____

HOW TO READ NEWSPAPER MUTUAL FUND TABLES

Exhibit 2-22 shows you how to read the mutual fund table in the newspaper. The first column is the fund's abbreviated name. Several funds listed under the same heading indicate a family of funds.

The second column, headlined "Sell," is the NAV price per share. You'll recall, the NAV is identified as the amount per share you would receive if you sold your shares (less deferred sales charges, if any). So on any given day, you can determine the value of your holdings by multiplying the NAV by the number of shares you own.

The third column, headlined "Buy," is the offering price (sometimes called the *asking* price). This is the price you would pay if you purchased shares that day. The buy price is the NAV, plus any sales charges. If the fund

EXHIBIT 2-22 Reading Newspaper Mutual Fund Tables

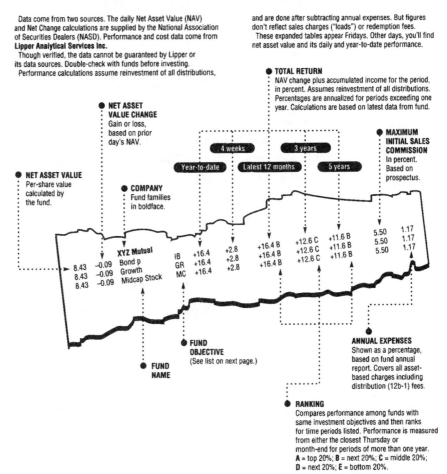

Data come from two sources. The daily Net Asset Value (NAV) and Net Change calculations are supplied by the National Association of Securities Dealers (NASD). Performance and cost data come from **Lipper Analytical Services Inc.**
Though verified, the data cannot be guaranteed by Lipper or its data sources. Double-check with funds before investing.
Performance calculations assume reinvestment of all distributions,

and are done after subtracting annual expenses. But figures don't reflect sales charges ("loads") or redemption fees.
These expanded tables appear Fridays. Other days, you'll find net asset value and its daily and year-to-date performance.

● **TOTAL RETURN**
NAV change plus accumulated income for the period, in percent. Assumes reinvestment of all distributions. Percentages are annualized for periods exceeding one year. Calculations are based on latest data from fund.

● **NET ASSET VALUE CHANGE**
Gain or loss, based on prior day's NAV.

● **MAXIMUM INITIAL SALES COMMISSION**
In percent. Based on prospectus.

● **NET ASSET VALUE**
Per-share value calculated by the fund.

● **COMPANY**
Fund families in boldface.

4 weeks   3 years
Year-to-date   Latest 12 months   5 years

XYZ Mutual

8.43	−0.09	Bond p	IB	+16.4	+2.8	+16.4 B	+12.6 C	+11.6 B	5.50	1.17
8.43	−0.09	Growth	GR	+16.4	+2.8	+16.4 B	+12.6 C	+11.6 B	5.50	1.17
8.43	−0.09	Midcap Stock	MC	+16.4	+2.8	+16.4 B	+12.6 C	+11.6 B	5.50	1.17

● **FUND OBJECTIVE**
(See list on next page.)

● **ANNUAL EXPENSES**
Shown as a percentage, based on fund annual report. Covers all asset-based charges including distribution (12b-1) fees.

● **FUND NAME**

● **RANKING**
Compares performance among funds with same investment objectives and then ranks for time periods listed. Performance is measured from either the closest Thursday or month-end for periods of more than one year.
A = top 20%; **B** = next 20%; **C** = middle 20%; **D** = next 20%; **E** = bottom 20%.

is a no-load, "NL" for no-load will appear in this column. The fourth column shows the change in NAV from the day before.

The Rating Game

The mutual fund rating game works much the same way as the old *Dating Game* on television. Investors use ratings of mutual funds that are listed in newspapers and magazines as a guide to help them pick funds that are the right ones for their portfolios.

Choosing an A-rated fund is a quick and easy way to choose a fund, but are these ratings actually useful? Let's consider mutual fund ratings in *The Wall Street Journal* as compiled by Lipper Analytical Services. Lipper awards an A to funds that have returns in the top 20 percent of their category. The next 20 percent get Bs and so on, through C, D, and E.

This means that the Vanguard Index 500 Fund is ranked in the top 20 percent of all similar funds, and the Vanguard Index Small Company Fund only ranks in the middle of its peer group. Likewise, for 1997 through 1999, the Vanguard Index European Fund managed the highest rating of A, while the Vanguard Index Pacific Fund only gets a D for the previous 12 months. So something is odd or wrong with these ratings.

Index funds are the easiest of all funds to rank; they simply mirror broad market segments and disclose exactly what's in their portfolios. Actively managed funds are much harder to classify than index funds because they have changing styles, fluctuating asset allocation, and other complications. If Lipper can't classify index funds correctly, how accurate can other ratings be? Good ratings bring money into mutual funds, bonuses to managers, and so on. Naturally, managers will do whatever they need to do to improve their ratings.

WHAT IF YOU'VE BOUGHT A BAD FUND?

What if you're in a mutual fund that isn't performing according to its underlying asset classes or your stated goals? We don't want to be going against our own advice on the subject of market timing, but this is an exception— sometimes you just buy a bad fund. Let's look at the telltale signs of a bad mutual fund:

- **Above Average Expenses**. Higher costs take a bigger bite out of the return earned by the stocks, meaning lower return to you. If your fund investment loses 3 percent, for example, and has a 2 percent annual expense ratio, you've actually sustained a 5 percent loss for the year. Lipper Analytical says the average stock mutual fund has an annual expense ratio of 1.54 percent. The average fixed income fund is around 0.96 percent. You can find the expense ratio in your fund's prospectus.

- **Poor Communication**. Troubled funds often fall behind on providing information in a timely fashion. If information isn't arriving on time, and you don't get a satisfactory explanation, it's appropriate to get nervous.

- **Lack of Discipline**. The best investments take a consistent approach. The worst type of funds pursue whatever is hot. If your fund has changed its focus, or if the manager has changed his or her style, the fund could be chasing a hot sector, trying to enhance returns.

- **Managers Change**. If the managers keep leaving, there's something going on. The fund owes you an adequate explanation. They need to tell you what the new guy can do to help turn it around.

- **Shrinking Assets**. This is the biggest indicator. Funds get bigger when they're making more money and they shrink when they lose. When investors lose confidence, the shrinking can be dramatic.

EXCHANGE TRADED FUNDS

Exchange traded funds (ETFs) are fast becoming an investment product worth paying attention to. These relatively new investments, affectionately called *spiders* and *diamonds*, already make up between 30 percent and 50 percent of the daily volume on the American Stock Exchange. Their importance is continuing to grow as leading institutions and large mutual funds plan their entry into the ETF market. Yet the real story behind the emergence of ETFs is the effect they'll have on mutual funds and retail investors.

Even a first time investor can make investing in ETFs a part of the decision-making process.

ETFs originally were designed by institutional investors to try to solve the discount or premium problem with closed-end funds. Organized as unit investment trusts, ETFs introduced an arbitrage mechanism. Instead of selling their shares to the public for cash, they continuously swap large blocks of ETF shares, primarily with institutional investors in amounts as low as $500,000 for in-kind securities plus cash representing mostly dividends. The large blocks of ETF shares are called *creation units*, which are swapped for portfolio deposits (the stock) and the cash component. Shares are redeemed in the same manner. Institutional investors are given shares from the ETF's portfolio in exchange for the redemption of the creation unit. In a relatively short time since their introduction, ETFs' popularity dwarfed that of closed-end funds.

There are advantages of ETFs over today's mutual funds. For one, ETFs are priced and traded throughout the day similar to shares of common stock. Although this might help traders, a more important feature is the tax treatment. Like mutual funds, ETFs are structured as regulated investment companies. This means that ETFs must distribute all income and realized gains to shareholders just like mutual funds. While mutual funds have recognized the problems with taxable distributions, their response has been to either tack on redemption fees, some for as long as five years, or emphasize tax-aware trading strategies that may be more marketing than substance. While they have an identical tax structure, ETFs have taken advantage of the rules for tax-efficiency that mutual funds haven't.

Unlike mutual funds that sell securities for cash to cover redemptions, ETFs transfer out securities in-kind. And although this doesn't occur when small investors redeem (they do so on the exchange with other investors), it does occur when larger institutions want to sell.

With a mutual fund, the accounting department identifies the lots of the securities sold and, in a partial sale, assigns the cost basis. Progressive mutual fund companies usually try to sell the highest long-term cost basis shares first. This method might initially delay the recognition of a capital gain, but in the case of a large redemption, the mutual fund would eventually generate a tax liability. The gains are ultimately distributed to the remaining shareholders. ETFs are different. In a large redemption, the ETF can identify which securities and how much of each will be distributed in-kind. The securities can be identical in proportion to the current ETF portfolio, or they can be different. Like mutual funds, the ETFs accounting department identifies the specific lots of these securities, but instead of selling the securities and realizing the gains, the shares are transferred to the redeeming investor. The accountants can assign the securities with the lowest cost basis, therefore continually washing away the unrealized tax liability. When tax-exempt institutional investors redeem, the tax liability effectively disappears.

Both mutual funds and ETFs have to sell shares when there are changes in the index. A recent example was the sale of Chrysler stock associated with the Daimler-Benz merger in 1999. Chrysler was dropped from the S&P 500, and index mutual funds had to realize capital gains. This is one reason the Vanguard Index 500 has already made a significant distribution for the first six months of 1999. Had it needed to, the SPDR may have been able to transfer out through redemption of the Chrysler shares, but with a low level of unrealized gains and a shorter time since inception, the transfer perhaps would not have been necessary. And in fact, this is another ETF advantage. ETFs don't have the accumulated gains for the past 15 plus years of a bull market.

NOTES: _____

_____

_____

_____

_____

INDIVIDUALLY MANAGED ACCOUNTS

An *individually managed account,* also known as a separately managed account, is a separate investment vehicle in which the investor gives full discretion over cash and/or securities to an investment firm to manage according to the client's specifications.

Individually managed accounts have similarities to mutual funds, such as professional management, cost, diversification, and liquidity. They differ because the portfolio manager buys securities specifically for the owner of the individual account. In a mutual fund, the portfolio manager cannot take into consideration individual investor nuances.

There are advantages of individually managed accounts over today's mutual funds. For one, you own all the individual securities in your account. Investments in a managed account are not pooled with those of other investors, as in a mutual fund. Plus individually managed account programs routinely handle specific and unique requests, such as tax considerations.

Following are other types of fee-based accounts:

- In a *client-directed, fee-based account,* the client directs the investments on a discretionary basis and can trade as much as he or she wants, but is only charged one fee. These accounts are rising in popularity and usually contain trading restrictions to control the frequency of trading.

- A *broker-directed account* or *personally advised account* is one for which the stockbroker directs the investments on a discretionary basis. There is no independent money manager. Pioneered at EF Hutton, these programs are usually available through only a limited number of very large, prequalified brokers.

- *Guided managed account programs* are brokerage accounts that use their research departments to put together "buy" lists and give broker-advisors a choice of one or two securities in each category for the clients. These programs are some of the fastest-growing products at many firms.

- *Mutual fund wraps,* also known as *mutual fund managed accounts,* consist of a portfolio of mutual funds with an added advisory fee. This was the hottest product in the 1990s, but has recently cooled down as diversified asset allocation has not performed well in the technology-heavy bull market.

The typical individual managed account manager has total costs of around 1.25 to 2.5 percent of the money under management. Mutual funds do not accommodate the large investor (over $500,000) as all investors pay their pro rata portion of the expenses. In a separate account however, larger invested amounts result in lower fees in proportion to assets invested. Some mutual funds have a variety of other so-called distribution charges while a separate

EXHIBIT 2-23 Comparison of Cost-Related Features Between Mutual Funds and Individually Managed Accounts

Cost-Related Features	Mutual Funds	Individually Managed Accounts—Direct Ownership
Wrap Expense	1–2%	0.5–1.5%
Expenses (excluding brokerage costs)	1.40%	1.00%
Expenses (including brokerage costs)	1.53%, average brokerage costs estimated at (0.13% for the 10 largest funds)	1.25%
Volume fee discounts	No, all investors pay same percentage rate of expense ratio	Yes, larger investors pay a proportionately smaller fee
Other Costs	12b-1, sales loads, redemption charges, and so on	None

account has no such charges. Exhibit 2-23 compares cost-related features of account types.

Tax Efficiency

The average domestic equity mutual fund has a 20 percent unrealized capital gain. This 20 percent unrealized capital gain means that an investor investing new money today in a fund could owe tax on a 20 percent gain that they have not benefited from.

This imposes an additional and unnecessary tax burden on investors (Exhibit 2-24). The individual managed account investor does not buy into this unwarranted tax liability because the individual managed account investor establishes his or her own cost basis at the time of purchase. In addition, the investor holds each security the portfolio manager purchases (Exhibit 2-25).

Additionally, in an individually managed account, investors can customize the construction of their portfolios well beyond the standard investment style differentiation. They can restrict specific securities from their portfolio. This capability enables them to control the diversification of their overall investment plan. For example, many investors have large positions in the stock of their employer, in their pension plan, their 401(k) plan, or stock options. Such investors may want to bar their money manager from holding any of that company's stock, or even from holding stocks of other companies in the same industry, in order to keep the diversification plan on track. In an individually managed portfolio, managers may handle such restrictions as a matter of routine. In a mutual fund, there is no mechanism to restrict a stock or industry.

Next, let's examine the kinds of assets that both equity mutual funds and individually managed account vehicles contain.

EXHIBIT 2-24 Comparison of Tax-Related Features Between Mutual Funds and Individually Managed Accounts

Tax-Related Features	Mutual Funds	Individually Managed Accounts—Direct Ownership
Separately Held Securities	NO, investor holds one security, the fund, which in turn owns a diversified portfolio	YES, investor holds securities in an account purchased by their portfolio manager
Unrealized Capital Gains	YES, average U.S. mutual fund has a 20% unrealized capital gain	NO, at the time of purchase the investor establishes his or her own cost basis for each security in the portfolio
Customized to Control Taxes	NO, most fund managers manage for pre-tax return without regard for the tax liability they may create for investors. All investors pay their proportionate share of taxes	YES, investors can instruct their portfolio manager to take gains or losses as available to manage their tax liability. Some managers will explicitly manage to control the tax consequences
Gain/Loss Distribution Policies	All gains distributed, losses cannot be distributed	Treated as direct stock ownership in which realized gains and losses are reported in the year recorded

EXHIBIT 2-25 Performance Reporting Features of Mutual Funds and Individually Managed Accounts

Performance Reporting Features	Mutual Funds	Individually Managed Accounts—Direct Ownership
Investor reporting	Typically semi-annual, some funds more frequent	Monthly statement of positions and transactions
Performance reporting	Typically semi-annual, some funds more frequent	Quarterly performance reporting
Customized Performance Reporting	NO, investors must calculate their own performance which is problematic particularly for investors who dollar cost average	YES, automatically sent to investors on a quarterly basis including performance of aggregate of multiple portfolios and the individual portfolios

INVESTING DIRECTLY IN STOCKS

Both equity mutual funds and individually managed account vehicles are made of many individual stocks. A stock, also known as an equity, is a security issued by a corporation as a means of raising long-term capital. The ownership is divided into a certain number of shares; the corporation issues stock certificates that show how many shares are owned. The stockholders own the company and elect a board of directors to manage it for them.

The capital a company raises through the initial sale of these shares entitles the new holder to dividends and to other rights of ownership, such as voting rights.

Prices of stocks change according to general business conditions and the earnings and future prospects of the companies that have issued the stock. If the business is doing well, stockholders may be able to sell their stock for a profit. If it is not, they may have to take a loss when they sell. The mutual fund manager picks stocks based on the objective of the fund.

Many investors are under the mistaken belief that companies make a profit if their shares rise in value. The only time a company keeps the capital is when it goes public by offering its stock for sale. When a company goes public, it does so in an initial public offering or IPO. Not only does selling stock on the market add to what is called the total capitalization of the company (the total number of shares multiplied by the share price), it also means the company will gain more capital when it issues a new offering of stock. When you buy stock, except for initial public offerings or new issues, the stock you buy through your broker is being sold to you by another investor, not by the corporation that originally issued it.

Large corporations may have many thousands of stockholders. Their stock is bought and sold in marketplaces called *stock exchanges*. A stock exchange occupies an important position in our country's financial system by providing a mechanism for converting savings into physical and portfolio investment. It also performs two major functions; it provides a primary or new-issues market, in which new capital can be raised by issuing financial securities; plus, a secondary market for trading existing securities that facilitates transferability of securities from sellers to buyers.

The shares of stock represent the value of the corporation. When the corporation has made a profit, the directors may divide the profit among stockholders as dividends, or they may decide to use it to expand the business. Dividends are paid to the stockholders out of the corporation's profits. When profits are used to expand the business, the directors and stockholders may issue more stock to show that there is more money invested in the business. This new stock will be divided among existing stockholders as stock dividends.

Breaking this down further, stocks are issued in two forms: common and preferred.

Common Stock

Common stock represents true ownership shares in a company. Stockholders share directly in growing company profits through increasing dividends and an appreciation in the value of the stock itself. As the holder of common stock, you are a part-owner in the company issuing the stock. The purchaser of common stock not only receives a share of any dividends paid by the corporation, but also gets the right to vote for corporate directors who, in turn, choose the corporate officers and set the corporation's policies. When an advisor uses the term stock, he or she is normally referring to *common* stock.

Preferred Stock

Preferred stock, like common stock, represents ownership or equity, and not debt. Preferred stockholders have a claim on profits which precedes—or is preferred to—the claim of the common-stock holder. The preferred-stock holder has a right to receive *specified* dividends (for example, 10 percent of the face value of the preferred share) before the common-stock holder can be paid any dividend at all.

On the other hand, the preferred-stock holder does not have the possibility of large gains open to the common-stock holder. While the common-stock holder may hope for rising dividends if the corporation prospers, the preferred-share holder will at most receive the specified dividend.

If the preferred stockholders share with the common-stock holders in dividends beyond the specified percentage, the stock is called *participating preferred*.

Preferred stock also may be cumulative. That is, if there are no dividends given in a year, the preferred-stock holders must be given double their dividend the next year. This is paid before anything is paid to the common-stock holders. This principle continues for as many years as dividends are not paid.

More tools are used to evaluate stock investments.

Price/Earnings Ratio

This is one way managers measure the value of a company. The price/earnings or P/E ratio measures the stock's price divided by the company's earnings per share (EPS) over the past 12 months. If a company is earning $1 a share and the public is buying the stock at $10, the market price is divided by the earnings. In this case, 10 is divided by 1; this tells us that the stock is selling at 10 times its earnings (10P/E or 10x).

If your manager invests in this company and is paid $10, theoretically he or she is paying 10 years' worth of earnings to own it. When the market is low, you will see stock prices at 10 times earnings. In a bull market, the average is 25 to 30 times earnings.

Dividend Payout Ratio Tool

This is the ratio of a company's indicated annual cash dividend per share to its EPS, and can range from 0 to 100 percent. A utility that pays out $4 in dividends for each $5 of earnings would have a payout of 80 percent. The payout is above 50 percent for the average large industrial company and even higher for the typical utility. The higher the dividend payout, however, the less room there is for dividend increases, since less profit is available to reinvest for future growth.

Dividend Yield Tool

This measures the annual dividend divided by the stock price. For example, if a utility's dividend is $4 and its stock sells for $50 a share, the yield would be 8 percent. When the EPS is high, yields will be low.

Blue-Chip Stocks

These high quality companies are typically large, old, and well established, such as those represented in the Dow Jones Industrial Average. Blue chips often are considered income stocks by virtue of their fairly high dividend payouts. Many of the companies included in the S&P 500 would also qualify as blue chips.

If you haven't the time or the inclination to research companies in which to invest, let a professional pick your stocks, either in a fund, or if you have enough money, in a separate account. With this approach, over the long run you will outperform the majority of those who engage in costly buying and selling done without a systematic selection process.

UNDERSTANDING FIXED INCOME SECURITIES

Every investment breaks down to either being a lender or an owner. The investment of the lender is called a bond or fixed income security.

Most first time investors don't understand what makes a bond different from all other types of investments. A bond is the legal evidence of a debt, usually the result of a loan of money.

When you buy a bond, you are, in effect, lending your money to the issuer of the bond. The issuer agrees to make periodic interest payments to you, the investor holding the bond, and also agrees to repay the original sum, the principal, in full to you on a certain date. This date is known as the bond's maturity date.

What backs the bond? In the case of many corporate securities, the full faith and credit of the companies that issue them. These bonds, usually called debentures, are probably the most common type of debt issued by industrial corporations today. Public utilities generally issue bonds with specific assets as collateral against the loan. These are called *mortgage* bonds or *collateral trust* bonds. Some utilities, however, issue debentures and some industrial corporations issue collateralized bonds.

INVESTING DIRECTLY IN BONDS

What Are the Risks?

The main form of market risk for a bond is the risk of interest rates changing after a customer buys the bond—called *interest-rate risk*. If market interest rates go up, the bond loses principal value; if market rates go down, the bond gains principal value. The longer the term of the bond, the more the price will be affected by changes in interest rates. Whether the U.S. government, a corporation, or a municipality issues the bond, the risk is similar.

Bonds are also subject to *call risk*, or, the risk that the bond issuer will choose to redeem the bond before the maturity date. The call provisions must be stated in the prospectus along with other special features. But, a prospectus can be hard to understand.

A Look at Interest Rates

A bond's current value is directly affected by changes in the interest rates. The effect of higher interest rates on bonds is to lower their prices. Conversely, lower rates raise bond prices. (See Exhibit 2-26.) The fluctuation is due to the fact that the price of the bond must offer a prospective purchaser current market rates.

When should an individual buy a bond, rather than a bond fund? There is a lot to understand before buying an individual bond. It is a somewhat dif-

EXHIBIT 2-26 Bond Price, Yield, and Interest Rates. A significant part of understanding bonds is the realization of the inverse relationship of a bond's cost (dollar price) to its yield. Higher bond yields result in lower dollar prices and declining yields raise dollar prices.

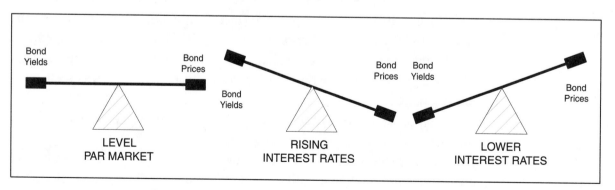

ferent process from buying stocks or mutual funds, because only a certain dollar amount of each bond is issued and that amount is almost certainly much smaller than the amount of equity issued. Large companies have millions of shares of stock outstanding, and all shares of common stock are the same. To buy a bond, on the other hand, the customer can't simply consult *The Wall Street Journal*, pick a particular bond, and place an order. Buying a bond means finding the owner, such as an institutional trading desk, of a bond that meets your needs.

Any institutional investor buys bonds more cheaply than a single individual; and the bonds in a mutual fund have been purchased at the institutional price. The institutional investor also pays a minuscule portion of total price in transaction costs, whereas transaction costs can be significant for an individual. It gets worse if the individual must pay for safekeeping the securities. A bond fund does, however, pay a management fee that might equal in yield the transaction cost an individual would pay.

Kinds of Individual Bonds That Make Up Fixed Income Asset Classes

There are three main categories of bonds:

1. The U.S. government or one of its agencies
2. Corporations
3. Municipals

While these types have some different characteristics, they share a basic structure.

U.S. Government Notes and Bonds. The U.S. government issues both Treasury notes (maturities of 2 to 10 years) and bonds (maturities over 10 years). U.S. government securities are considered to have no credit risk, and their rate of return is the benchmark that all other rates of return in the market are compared to. The government auctions U.S. government securities on a regular quarterly schedule.

Corporate Bonds. These are largely what you find inside a bond or balanced fund. Corporations of every size and credit quality issue corporate bonds, from the very best blue-chip companies to small companies with low ratings. Corporate bonds are not easy to evaluate, especially those with longer maturities, when call provisions may apply and the credit outlook is less certain.

Yields are higher on corporate bonds than on a CD or government-issued or insured debt. The coupon is fixed and return of principal is guaranteed by the issuer if the investor holds it until maturity. If the investor sells the bond prior to maturity, the bond will be subject to market fluctuations. Investors who want to be able to check the prices of their bonds in the newspaper should buy listed bonds, preferably those listed on the New York Stock Exchange.

The fully taxable nature of corporate bonds, as opposed to municipals or Treasuries has an effect on yield. When buying an AAA-rated corporate bond, you are buying a security that has more risk than a U.S. government bond. For the risk you are taking, you should receive an additional 25 to 50 basis points in yield.

Municipal Bonds. Municipal bonds are investment instruments used to finance municipal governmental activities.

Mutual fund managers whose goal is simply to conserve capital and generate returns that keep up with inflation, often look to municipal bonds with the idea that these bonds are fairly safe. Investors may believe this because *munis* issuances often have language stating they are "backed by the full faith and credit" of the issuing authority. In addition to the safety that conservative investors think they are gaining in municipal bonds, investors may also believe that these bonds' tax-free status offers additional rewards. The combination of safety and tax-advantaged reward seems irresistible to many who are not especially sophisticated about the securities markets and who seek to avoid making an investment mistake.

Municipals attract many wealthy investors for the reasons stated above. They're not looking for growth, they've already made it. The largest part of Ross Perot's holdings are in municipal bonds. I'm sure if we asked him, he'd say he's not concerned about growth. But then again, who knows what Perot would say.

Information to Review Before Making a Bond Purchase

What follows is information a mutual fund manager would look at before making a bond purchase:

- **Security Description**. Type of bond, purpose of the bond, and the issuer.
- **Rating**. For example, AA is better than A.
- **Trade Date**. Date the bond is purchased in the market.
- **Settlement Date**. The date the purchaser pays for the bond and interest starts accruing.
- **Maturity Date**. The date the purchaser will be repaid the principal and last interest payment.

- **Interest Payment Dates**. Dates interest payments are made, usually semi-annually.

- **Coupon**. Fixed annual interest rate (interest income) stated on the bond.

- **Price**. Dollar price paid for the bond. An offer price is the price at which the individual investor buys the bond. The bid price is the price at which the individual can sell the bond.

- **Current Yield**. The coupon divided by price, giving a rough approximation of cash flow.

- **Yield to Maturity**. Measure of total return on the bond at maturity.

- **Par Amount**. Face amount of the bond when it was issued, normally $1,000.

- **Accrued Interest**. The amount of interest income (coupon income) earned from the date of the last coupon payment to settlement date.

- **Basis.** Whether the bond uses a 360-day or 365-day basis to calculate interest payments.

Bond Rating Services. A mutual fund manager also looks at the findings of the bond rating services. The two major independent rating services are Moody's and Standard & Poor's.

Investment-grade ratings range from AAA to BBB– (Standard & Poor's), or Aaa to Baa3 (Moody's). Lower-rated bonds are considered speculative. Ratings are intended to help you evaluate risk and set your own standards for investment.

Exhibit 2-27 shows some bond rating schemes. Grades AAA through BBB are considered investment grade, although many mutual fund managers confine their attention to bonds rated A or above. Ratings attempt to assess the probability that the issuing company will make timely payments of interest and principal. Each rating service has slightly different evaluation methods.

EXHIBIT 2-27 Bond Ratings

Credit Risk	Moody's	S&P
Excellent	Aaa, Aa	AAA, AA
Upper Medium	A-1, A	A+, A
Lower Medium	Baa-1, baa, a	BBB+, BBB
Speculative	Ba	BB
Very Speculative	B, Caa	B, CCC, CC
Default	Ca, C	DDD, DD, D

INVESTMENT VEHICLES THAT ARE SHELTERED FROM TAX

The IRS imposes no limits on the annual nonsheltered amount an individual may contribute into what is called a variable annuity—it is funded with after-tax dollars. In other words, you can put in as much money as you can afford. This is particularly important when it comes to supplementing retirement assets beyond the annual tax-free contribution limitation.

What can you put your money in once you've maximized your retirement vehicles? In general, there are two types of annuities, fixed and variable. A fixed annuity provides a specific income for life. With a variable annuity, payouts are dependent on investment return, which is not guaranteed. Variable annuities offer the choice of several investment divisions such as stocks, bonds, and money market funds, which can cause the rate of return to fluctuate with market conditions.

In both fixed and variable annuities, you do not have to pay income tax on the accumulated earnings until payouts start. But you should keep in mind that withdrawals are taxable and, if you are under age $59\frac{1}{2}$, may be subject to a 10 percent tax penalty.

Fixed Annuities

The fixed annuity offers security in that the rate of return is certain. Typically, with a fixed annuity the insurance company declares a current interest rate and sets the interest rate.

The fixed aspect of the annuity also offers security in that the annuity holder does not take responsibility for making decisions about how the money should be invested. The amount of the benefit that will be paid out of the annuity when the contract is annuitized is fixed.

Example: A customer has accumulated $50,000 in an annuity. He owns a 6 percent fixed annuity and wants to make consistent monthly payments over the next 15 years. He can plan on payments of $421 each month to the annuity. At his retirement, his original $50,000 lump sum will grow to approximately $76,000.

NOTES: _____

_____

_____

_____

Variable Annuities

Variable annuities are often called "mutual funds with an insurance wrapper." A variable annuity combines the best aspects of a traditional fixed annuity including tax deferral, insurance protection for beneficiaries, tax timing controlled income options, with the benefits of traditional mutual fund type portfolios including flexibility in selecting how to invest funds and the potential for higher investment returns.

Example: Let's say you are a 35-year-old investing $10,000 in a low cost, tax-deferred variable annuity, and you're fortunate to get a return of 12 percent. By your 65th birthday, you could accumulate over $240,000. If you are able to add $5,000 a year all along the way, your $160,000 of total invested capital, compounding tax free, could balloon to over $1,282,558. If you continue working and don't retire until age 70, your variable annuity could hold over $2,224,249. That's what's possible by investing in a variable annuity.

NOTES: _____

_____

_____

_____

Variable annuity investors control their contract options. They dictate the amount, frequency, and regularity of their contributions, how their contributions are invested, and when the money is disbursed. The investor pays a premium to the insurance company, which then buys *accumulation units*, similar to mutual fund shares, in an investment fund.

The variable annuity investor directs those funds in subaccount portfolios consisting of stocks, bonds, or cash money market funds. Diverse investment options make it possible to structure an investment portfolio to meet a variety of needs, goals, and risk tolerances. These investments may be managed by a mutual fund company or by the insurance company. With the important advantage of tax-free rebalancing, investors can adjust their portfolios at any time. This allows an investor's advisor to carefully plan and manage the asset-allocation strategy based on changing needs or market conditions, without having to worry about generating current tax.

Investing in a Tax-Deferred Annuity

Unlike a mutual fund, an annuity does not pay out earnings or distribute any capital gains, so these are compounded on a tax-deferred basis. The ability to reallocate assets without current tax ramifications, combined with the tax-deferred compounding of potential earnings, makes variable annuities a highly competitive investment vehicle.

A variable annuity's rate of return is determined by the performance of the investments selected. As the value of the stocks in the portfolio varies, each unit will be worth more or less. Today's variable annuity managers, along with their affiliate mutual fund managers, seek diversification, consistent performance, and competitive returns by maximizing a portfolio's return and also minimizing the level of risk. Variable annuity investments are often balanced by investing a percentage of assets in the annuity fixed income option to provide a less volatile investment return.

The amount of variable payments is not guaranteed or fixed and may decrease in periods of market decline. However, if the annuitant dies during the accumulation phase, that is, prior to receiving payments from the annuity, the investor's designated beneficiary is guaranteed to receive the greater of the account's accumulated value, or the full amount invested less any withdrawals and applicable premium taxes.

When withdrawals do begin, taxes generally are paid only on the amounts withdrawn that represent a gain at ordinary tax rates, while the remainder of the account value can continue to grow tax-deferred. However, if the investor takes funds from the annuity before age $59\frac{1}{2}$, there is the additional 10 percent IRS penalty on the withdrawal of any gain.

Most variable annuities offer a free annual withdrawal provision that gives the investor access of up to 10 percent of the annuity value yearly without paying any surrender charges. Any distributions in excess of that 10 percent are subject to surrender charges. No-load variable annuities that do not impose a surrender charge are 100 percent liquid but, like all annuities, may be subject to a 10 percent federal penalty for withdrawal prior to age $59\frac{1}{2}$.

Despite their inherent advantages, all variable annuities are *not* created equal. They can vary widely in terms of cost and available investment options. Because of their insurance benefits, variable annuities generally cost more than traditional taxable investments, such as mutual funds. There may be front-end charges, or loads, management fees, and back-end surrender charges for early withdrawals from the policy. These charges and the length of time they apply to the policy vary widely across the industry. The average policy probably has a 6 to 7 percent first-year surrender charge that declines one percentage point per year. Some have *rolling* surrender charges which means that each investment you make has a new surrender charge schedule.

In addition to portfolio management fees, variable annuities charge a fee to cover the issuing insurance company's administrative costs and mortality and expense (M&E) charges. According to Morningstar Benchmarks, annual M&E charges for the industry average in 2001 are around 1.3 percent and are increasing.

The higher the overall costs, the longer it takes for the benefit of tax deferral to compensate for those costs. In general, variable annuities are designed to be held as long-term investment vehicles so a break-even of 10 to 15 years may be affordable for those investors with that type of time frame.

In a variable annuity, the annuity holder may choose how to allocate premium dollars among a number of investment choices including stocks, bonds, a guaranteed account, income, growth fund, and various funds called subaccounts.

A subaccount is a term that describes the mutual fund portfolio held inside a variable annuity.

Variable annuities offer anywhere from 5 to 35 subaccount investment options. Mutual fund account managers select individual securities inside the subaccounts; the investor then selects the most appropriate subaccount based on the security selection for his or her portfolio. If this sounds exactly like a mutual fund, that's because it is. The same, or *clone* as they're commonly called, mutual funds tend to have the same managers inside variable annuity subaccounts, so the same criteria exist for choosing a mutual fund as for choosing a subaccount—and the same benefits also exist, such as professional money management, convenience, economies of scale, and diversification.

Types of Subaccounts. Subaccounts may be divided into several broad categories among asset classes (see Exhibit 2-28):

1. Aggressive growth
2. Stable growth
3. Balanced
4. Fixed income
5. Money market rates

In each of these classes, categories are further broken down.

Think of a subaccount inside the variable annuity and a mutual fund as being the same thing. Although they are kept separate, and the fund within each cannot be commingled, for ease of understanding how these work, we look at the predecessor to the subaccount—the mutual fund.

EXHIBIT 2-28 Typical Variable Annuity Investment Options

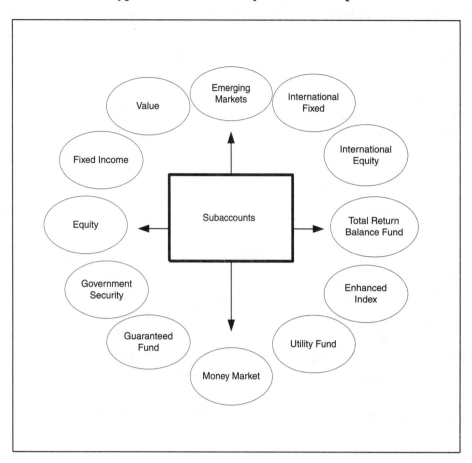

Methods of Purchase

1. **Single Premium Annuity.** A single premium annuity (see Exhibit 2-29) requires an initial lump-sum deposit (generally a minimum of $1,000 to $5,000) and does not accept any future contributions.

   As an example, Bob Jones recently received a settlement from an insurance claim—a lump sum of $150,000. He does not need the money currently, so he uses the funds to purchase a single premium annuity for $150,000 and chooses to receive benefits at his retirement age by electing one of the income settlement options.

   Other types of individuals might be athletes, actors, or artists who receive a large payment at one time. They purchase a single premium annuity that begins paying benefits when the person's career ends. Another example is a business owner who's recently sold his or her company. Once a single premium annuity has been purchased, the annuity holder can choose to begin receiving the benefit payments from the annuity at any time. If it is

EXHIBIT 2-29 Single Premium Annuity Accumulation Phase

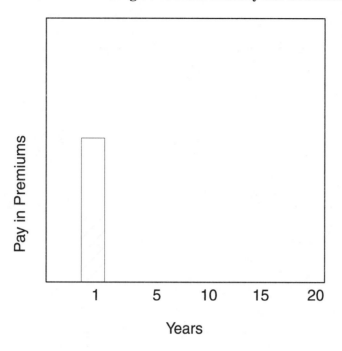

an immediate annuity, benefit payments will usually begin within one year of the annuity's purchase. However, if the annuity is a deferred annuity, the annuity holder may delay the receipt of benefits for several years.

2. **Flexible Premium Annuity.** A flexible premium annuity (see Exhibit 2-30) allows payments to be made at varying intervals and in varying amounts. Flexible premium annuities can accept future contributions and often require a smaller initial deposit. This type of annuity is usually used for accumulating a sum of money that will provide benefits at some point in the future. As with a single premium annuity, the flexible premium annuity also can purchase either a fixed or variable annuity.

Annuity Stages. There are two phases of an annuity:
1. The asset-building, or accumulation, phase
2. The payout, distribution, or benefit phase

A variable annuity is generally more appropriate for a customer with longer time horizons to allow a substantial accumulation of wealth through equity investments on a tax-deferred basis.

In the accumulation phase, you buy units similar to those of mutual fund shares. But unlike a mutual fund, the annuity does not pay out income or dis-

EXHIBIT 2-30 Flexible Premium Annuity Accumulation Phase

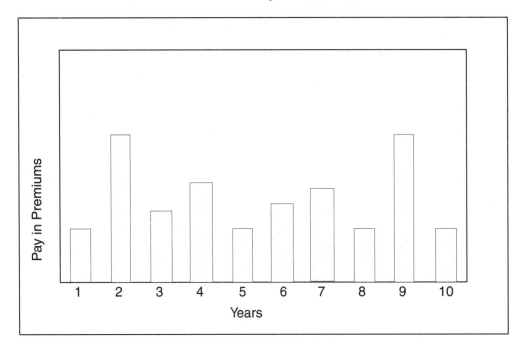

tribute any capital gains, so the customer accumulates unit values over a period of years. These also grow tax-deferred, making the compound effect even more dramatic.

The payout phase is when the insurance company starts making a series of payments consisting of principal and earnings for a defined period of time to the annuitant or to the main beneficiary. Taxes are only assessed on the portion of each payment that comes from earned interest except with qualified contracts.

The following payout options are:

- **Lifetime Income**. The entire account value is converted to a monthly income stream guaranteed for as long as the annuitant lives.

- **Lifetime Income with Period Certain**. Income stream is guaranteed for a specified number of years, or for as long as the annuitant lives, whichever is longer.

- **Refund Life Annuity**. The entire account value is converted to a monthly income stream guaranteed for as long as the annuitant lives. If the annuitant dies prior to the principal amount being annuitized, the balance is paid to the beneficiary.

- **Joint and Survivor**. Income stream is guaranteed for as long as either annuitant lives, for example, you or your spouse.

- **Fixed Period Certain**. The entire account value is fully paid out during a specified period of time.
- **Fixed Amount Annuity**. Equal periodic installments are withdrawn until the account balance is exhausted.

Death Benefits. If the annuitant dies, the value of the death benefit is the greater of the amount originally invested in the contract or the annuity's account value. The death benefit is guaranteed never to be lower than the total amount invested in the annuity. In this sense, annuities look a bit like life insurance.

Interest Rates. Typically, a fixed annuity contract will offer two interest rates: a guaranteed rate and a current rate.

The guaranteed rate is the minimum rate that will be credited to the funds in the annuity contract regardless of how low the current rate sinks or how poorly the insurance company fares. Typically, the guaranteed rate is 3 to 4 percent.

If you are considering the purchase of an annuity, you should ask:

- What is the current interest rate and how often does it change?
- Is there a "bailout option" that permits you to cash in the annuity, without withdrawal penalties (there may be tax penalties), if the interest rate drops below a specific figure?
- Are there front-end load charges or annual administrative fees? How much are they and how will they affect your return?

Conclusion. The variable annuity appears to be the answer to the shortfall retirement problems of longer life expectancies and longer retirement periods. Why? Because current trends point to drastic reductions in expected pension benefits, as both corporations and government are getting out of the retirement benefits business.

NOTES: _____

_____

_____

_____

_____

RETIREMENT PLAN VEHICLES

The IRS imposes limits on the amount an individual may contribute to a retirement plan with before-tax dollars. The important thing to remember is that all the asset class investment vehicles we have mentioned may be purchased inside the plans listed below. See Exhibit 2-31 for how tax-deferred investments accumulate.

Simplified Employee Pension

A simplified employee pension (SEP) allows you to make contributions toward your own (if you are self-employed) and your employees' retirement without getting involved in a more complex qualified plan.

You make the contributions to a traditional individual retirement arrangement (called a SEP-IRA) set up by or for each eligible employee. SEP-IRAs are owned and controlled by the employee, and you make contributions to the financial institution where the SEP-IRA is maintained.

EXHIBIT 2-31 Tax-Deferred Accumulation—A Powerful Financial Tool

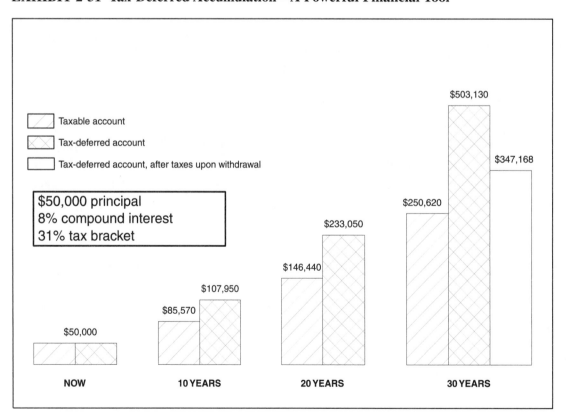

KEOGH Qualified Plans (Keogh Plans)

A qualified employer plan set up by a self-employed individual is sometimes called a Keogh or HR-10 plan. A sole proprietor or a partnership can set up a qualified plan that must exist for the exclusive benefit of employees or their beneficiaries.

As an employer, you can usually deduct, subject to limits, contributions you make to a qualified plan, including those made for your own retirement. The contributions, and earnings and gains on them, are generally tax-free until distributed by the plan.

Put more aggressive funds and asset classes inside your retirement plans. Turnover and capital gains can cut into your returns, but not in a retirement plan.

There's been a movement away from employer-pays-all plans, such as defined benefit plans, to employee-deferral plans, such as SEP-IRAs, 401(k)s, and SIMPLE plans.

SIMPLE Plans

A Savings Incentive Match Plan for Employees (SIMPLE) provides you and your employees a simplified way to make contributions to provide retirement income. Under a SIMPLE plan, employees can choose to make salary reduction contributions to the plan rather than receiving these amounts as part of their regular pay. In addition, you contribute matching or nonelective contributions.

A SIMPLE plan can take the form of a SIMPLE IRA or a 401(k) plan. Under a SIMPLE IRA plan, a SIMPLE IRA must be set up for each eligible employee.

401(k) Plans

A 401(k) allows employees to defer a portion of their income up to a certain percentage. That income, often matched by the employer up to a certain percentage, is excluded from the employees' reported earnings and is free from federal and state income taxes but not FICA-Social Security. When employers match their employees' contributions, they're actually giving the employees a bonus.

Traditional Individual Retirement Accounts (IRAs)

Some basics: IRAs, like 401(k)s and 403(b)s, are tax-advantaged vehicles. Usually this means you can defer taxes—put them off to a future date when your tax rate might be lower—but occasionally it means something else. With a Roth IRA, for example, you can contribute after-tax money and watch it grow tax-free. Rarely does the federal government let you escape taxes forever, so an important thing to know about any savings vehicle is the tax angle and how best to play it.

A traditional IRA is any IRA that is not a Roth IRA, a SIMPLE IRA, or an education IRA. You can set up a traditional IRA at any time, although the period for making contributions for any year is limited. As soon as you set up your traditional IRA, you can make contributions to it through your chosen sponsor, trustee, or other administrator. Contributions must be in the form of money, that is, cash, check, or money order. Property cannot be contributed. However, you may be able to transfer or roll over certain property from one retirement plan to another.

Roth IRAs

Too many people, young and old, who qualify for a Roth IRA are missing the boat. You can open a Roth IRA, and make contributions to it, at any age, and if you meet the eligibility requirements, you should jump at the chance. Some people shy away from this option because it doesn't offer a tax deduction. Big deal! If you are in the 28 percent tax bracket, a tax deduction on a $2,000 traditional IRA contribution is worth only $560 a year to you. That's only a little more than $10 a week, not enough even to take you and a friend to the movies. If you hold the Roth for at least five years, and until you reach 59½ years old, all distributions from that account will be tax-free for life. Plus, they'll be tax-free to your Roth IRA beneficiaries.

To qualify for the annual $2,000-per-person ($4,000 if married and filing jointly), Roth contribution, you must have earnings of at least $2,000 ($4,000 if married and filing jointly), and your income cannot exceed $95,000 ($150,000 for a couple) per year. At the point where your income exceeds $110,000 ($160,000 for a couple), you no longer qualify for a Roth. Between those limits, you qualify for a partial Roth contribution.

CONCEPTS THAT ARE LEAST EFFECTIVE

Are there more advanced investment strategies? Yes, but these strategies require more skill and years of experience. Most first time investors should avoid doing these by themselves.

Picking Individual Stocks

All investments have two risk components: systematic risk, otherwise known as market risk, and unsystematic risk, known as issue specific risk, or the risk inherent in any one specific investment. As investors look for higher returns, they have been enticed into buying individual stocks. Most do not understand the huge risk they are taking. Many of the rules used successfully in mutual funds do not work in individual stocks. Declines in individual stocks in 2000 were far worse than in any one fund. Declines often don't reverse for long periods of time, so buying on the dips doesn't always work. But buying a basket of individual stocks removes almost all the issue specific risk. Buying individual stocks is, in fact, a more advanced strategy and commands more study.

Don't waste time scanning the stock pages to try to find the next Microsoft. You are as likely to pick a loser as you are to pick a winner. All you need to do to be a successful investor is to participate in the free market system and its creation of wealth. You can accomplish this by owning a broadly diversified portfolio of equity securities. Let a professional select your stocks, either in a fund, or if you have enough money, in a separate account. With this approach, over the long run you will outperform the majority of those who engage in costly buying and selling.

Timing the Market

Successful market timing requires more than clairvoyance; it also demands nerves of steel. The very best time to buy is when prices have been falling for weeks or months and the market looks absolutely awful. The very best time to sell is the moment when the market is performing superbly. Not surprisingly, few people can bring themselves to do either.

Market timing is the attempt to be in the market when it goes up and out of the market when it goes down. Market-timers have to be right twice. First, they must get out of a particular market before it declines. Then they must get back in early enough to catch the next market rise.

On the contrary, most people much prefer to put money into a market that has been booming for a reassuringly long time and they tend to sell investments after the market has been falling.

People often will buy last year's top performer, then last year's top performer will lag and they'll sell it. They'll either take a loss or reduce their gain significantly, and then they'll go to the next high performer. Basically, they're moving their portfolios around way too much, and often incurring negative tax consequences as a result.

 Investors tend to invest after prices have gone up and sell after prices have gone down, when they should be doing the exact opposite. The difficult part of investing is to understand how to keep your greed and your fear in balance. Let's look at what happens when they can't.

The Emotional Roller Coaster

Exhibit 2-32 shows the ups and downs of investing emotionally. You hear about a hot new mutual fund or stock from a friend or business associate. You may get mildly excited, but hold back until you talk with your broker or financial planner. You flip through the paper, hoping that the mutual fund is going to go up and that a distinct trend will become evident. Let's say the fund does continue to go up and your hope turns to real excitement. It feels as if you've made a discovery! Greed strikes. What do you do next?

At this point, many of us call our broker or advisor and purchase the stock. But, as is often the case with hot tips, as soon as you purchase the stock, it goes down! Many investors have developed the belief that they can cause any security to go down by purchasing it. Now what is his or her emo-

EXHIBIT 2-32 The Emotional Curve of Investing

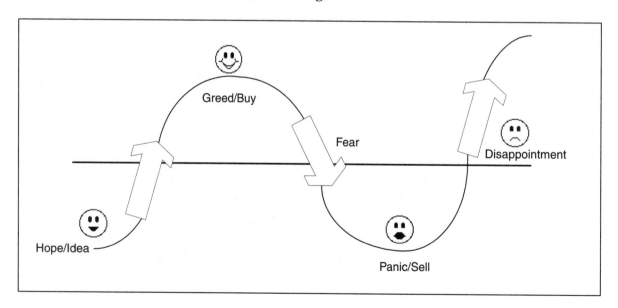

tion? Often, it is a combination of fear and hope. What are you hoping for? That the fund will go back up? How far up? You would be happy if it just went back up to where it was when you bought it and you could break even and not have to tell anyone about your misadventure. You vow never to do it again! But the stock continues to go down. What do you do now? Panic! Most investors sell at this point.

What happens next? Some new information comes out and the stock hits an all time high! Now, that's an emotional roller coaster ride that is familiar to all of us. If you continue investing based on your emotions, to buy high and sell low over a long period of time, you can do significant damage to yourself and your investment program. There's a better way.

Momentum Investing

Momentum proponents ride trends to buy stocks with strong upward price momentum. Company fundamentals are secondary to the analysis of a stock's growth curve. The key here is getting in on time. If you can catch the momentum, then your returns will grow. If you are in too late, then returns can stall.

Contrarian

A contrarian investor does the opposite of what most investors are doing at any particular time. According to contrarian opinion, if everyone is certain that something is about to happen, it won't.

It is possible to significantly reduce the risk of your investments by using options. We do not recommend that a first time investor do this without professional supervision. Options, or derivatives, can be very powerful, or very dangerous if not implemented in a professional manner.

In Section Three we find out how to implement a strategy.

Three

APPLYING A DISCIPLINED STRATEGY

 In this section we're going to match up the returns you expect to make with appropriate investment vehicles based on what you have discovered about yourself.

COMPLETING YOUR INVESTMENT POLICY STATEMENT

We started Section One by filling in the six steps of your investment policy statement. In Section Two we covered the rules and types of investments you should use in your investment portfolio. We're now going to fill out the balance of your IPS and discuss what your appropriate investment strategy should be.

We are also going to establish a target rate of return and any other restrictions you feel necessary. This IPS can also be used to provide specific instructions to an investment counselor or advisor and to cover such areas as target rates of return, risk tolerance, and desired holding periods of asset classes.

Now that you have had a chance to look at different investment rates of return and their risk levels, what is a reasonable rate of return you should expect for each of the three buckets of money?

WHAT'S A REASONABLE GROWTH RATE OF RETURN?

A general rule of thumb is that if you take the decline level that you are comfortable with as a quarterly decline and divide that percentage in half, the result is a reasonable rate of growth over a three-to-five-year period. If the result is less than 7, add a conservative money market rate of 3 to 4 percent. We do this to account for the fact that risk is nonlinear. This is a general rule that can give a simple overview of expected return.

For instance, if you are willing to take a 10 percent decline quarterly, divide that number in half (5 percent) and add 3 to 4 percent; a reasonable rate of growth that you can expect to capture is 8 to 9 percent annually over a three-to-five-year period. For example, if you discovered from the Lifeboat Drill in Section One that you can take up to a 25 percent decline, then your goal would be an investment that would capture 12.5 percent. Rule of thumb, divide the decline by two.

$$\frac{25\%}{2} = 12.5\%$$

EXHIBIT 3-1 Returns and the Level of Decline

Level of Decline (%)	Target Growth Rate (%)	Approximate Time Frame	Core Strategy	Riskometer
3	3–5	0–6 months	CDs, cash, money markets	
6	5–6	3–12 months	Bond fund, money markets, CDs, cash	
8	6–8	6 mos.–2 yrs.	Conservative balanced portfolio, bonds or bond funds, portfolio 1	
10	8–9	18 mos.–3 yrs.	Balanced fund, portfolio 2	
15	9–11	3–5 years	Conservative equity fund, portfolio 3	
23	10–13	5–7 years	Equity fund, portfolio 4	
35	11–14	5–10 years	Equities, portfolio 4	
50	12–15	5–10 years	Equities, portfolio 4	

It is important to note that there will sometimes be periods when you will experience declines in excess of this amount, and your returns might be superior at other times. These are just rules of thumb.

What Is a Reasonable Expected Return Based On Your Decline Level?
Exhibit 3-1 shows what a reasonable expected growth rate over a three-to-five-year period is based on your decline level, column one. Your growth rate is going to be a direct result of your willingness to take risk and the realization of the long-term nature of your investment objectives. In the core strategy we have identified portfolios that we describe in the next section. As you target higher growth, results become much less predictable.

 Go back to your IPS on pages 7–9 and reread question 1 for each of the three money drills. What level of decline can you tolerate? (Remember our Lifeboat Drill.) Write down a range of returns that would be appropriate for you. You can use this range of returns for each risk level as the framework to determine your return expectation for your portfolio, as well as for the component asset classes. Now fill in Question 7 of the IPS for each of the three money drills.

Your Target Growth Rate Short-Term _____

Your Target Growth Rate Mid-Term _____

Your Target Growth Rate Long-Term _____

Make sure that your target growth rate aligns with the time horizon and risk profile you completed in your IPS.

NOTES: _____

_____

_____

_____

_____

_____

Before we can accurately calculate your growth rate, you need to calculate the impact of taxes, especially when investing nonqualified money, for example, money that is not in an IRA or a 401(k). After you've read over the impact of taxes, we construct several portfolios ranging from conservative to aggressive.

THE IMPACT OF TAXES

To show the importance of the impact of taxes, we have calculated the impact of $100 invested, growing at 10 percent per year assuming the investor paid short-term gains every year at the maximum federal level (39.6 percent) and did not pay any state taxes (see Exhibit 3-2).

Obviously, many people will pay less in federal income taxes and pay additional amounts in state taxes, but this is just to illustrate the impact of taxes. If you have 100 percent short-term tax realization, you will only capture 6.4 percent at the end of a year. And, over the course of 20 years, your $100, instead of growing to nearly $600, grows to only $323. If you managed to defer your gains so that they were all long-term in nature instead, and therefore paid 20 percent in capital gains taxes, that shift alone would increase

EXHIBIT 3-2 Tax Efficiency Increases After-Tax Wealth. The returns shown represent annualized after-tax returns. This hypothetical illustration assumes a constant rate of return; under normal conditions your rate of return will fluctuate, which will affect the final value of your account. This example is based on current tax rates.

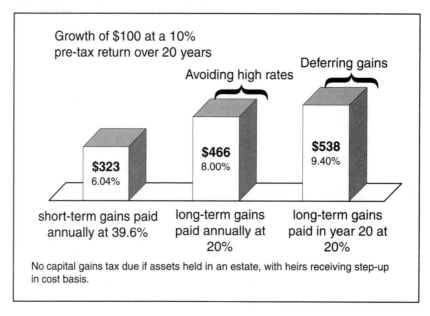

your return from 6.4 percent to 8 percent, and increase your after-tax growth by about 50 percent, to $466, over the course of 20 years. This illustrates the importance of deferring taxable gains in nonqualified or non-tax-deferred investments. A typical mutual fund has about 100 percent turnover, which means that you are paying taxes somewhere in between these two levels.

If you wanted to capture 10 percent after taxes, you would need to target different levels of growth depending on the taxes you would realize. For example, if you were turning your portfolio over and 100 percent of your gains were short-term in nature and you were in the maximum tax bracket, you would need to capture 16.5 percent growth to end up with 10 percent after taxes (see Exhibit 3-3). If, however, you wanted to end up with 10 percent and you managed to defer all your gains so they were long-term in nature (over 12 months), you would only need to capture 12.5 percent. Obviously, by reducing your tax realization, you can invest more conservatively and have a higher probability of capturing your desired after-tax returns.

Owning individual stocks, either by having a separate account portfolio, or by having individual stocks bought on your behalf, puts control of taxes in your hands. Mutual funds, by their design, do not place any control of tax issues in your hands. This does not mean they don't have their place—you just have no control.

EXHIBIT 3-3 Tax-Blind Investing Demands Exceptional Pre-Tax Returns.
The returns shown represent annualized after-tax returns. This hypothetical illustration assumes a constant rate of return; under normal conditions your rate of return will fluctuate, which will affect the final value of your account. This example is based on current tax rates.

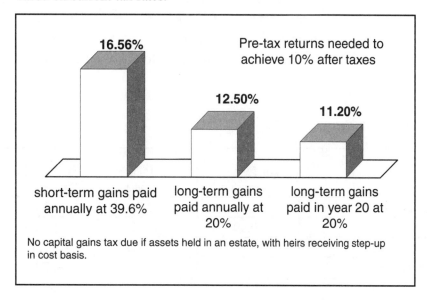

Pre-tax returns needed to achieve 10% after taxes

16.56% — short-term gains paid annually at 39.6%

12.50% — long-term gains paid annually at 20%

11.20% — long-term gains paid in year 20 at 20%

No capital gains tax due if assets held in an estate, with heirs receiving step-up in cost basis.

WHAT INVESTMENTS ARE APPROPRIATE?

In this section we outline several portfolios ranging from conservative to aggressive. These model portfolios use basic allocations that we wanted to give you as guideposts—a professional advisor might certainly do something more sophisticated.

Exhibit 3-4 is based on a buy-and-hold strategy and does not include the impact of taxes or expenses of any kind. Typically, if you buy index funds, you will reduce these numbers by about 50 basis points. These results are based on the years from 1970 to 2000.

The reason we chose to average the worst four quarters is because it takes out some of the really horrendous periods that occurred and distills them to an average. The same is true with the average of the worst four years; this way you get a realistic expectation of what a really bad year could look like, so you could expect to experience a decline of this magnitude and not be too surprised. Of course, it could be a little worse, or not as bad.

You will notice that these results are quite high, since we have gone through an amazing market where both bonds and stocks have done extremely well over the period 1990–2000.

When looking at these results, you would do well to figure in a reduction of 2 to 3 percent over a five-year period since we're clearly at the high end of the typical range of results expected for these portfolios. It's always better to be pleasantly surprised than disappointed.

It's surprising to notice how a small increase in the internal rate of return creates significant increases in risk.

Beta measures a stock or portfolio's volatility compared to the market as a whole. The Standard & Poor's 500 is used as the benchmark for measuring the beta of a stock or portfolio. If the benchmark is 1.0, a beta of 1.1 indicates that your stock is 10 percent more volatile than the market. A beta of 0.9 indicates that your stock is 10 percent less volatile than the market as a whole.

EXHIBIT 3-4 Four Portfolios

	Portfolio 4 Aggressive	Portfolio 3 Growth	Portfolio 2 Balanced	Portfolio 1 Conservative
Rate of Return, %	14.2	13.2	12.2	11
Beta	0.99	0.82	0.65	0.48
Average Worst 4 Qtrs., %	−15.6	−12.22	−8.9	−6
Average Worst 4 Yrs., %	−20	−16.3	−12	−8.3

NOTES: _____

_____

_____

_____

_____

_____

_____

_____

PORTFOLIO 1—CONSERVATIVE

EXHIBIT 3-5a

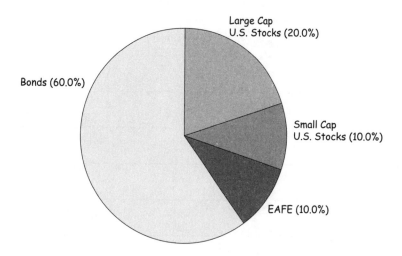

Target 5-year growth rate: 7–9%

Total rate of return since 1970: 11%

Beta: 0.48

Average of four worst quarters: –6%

Average of four worst years: –8.3%

NOTES: _____

_____

_____

_____

_____

_____

PORTFOLIO 2—BALANCED

RISKOMETER

EXHIBIT 3-5b

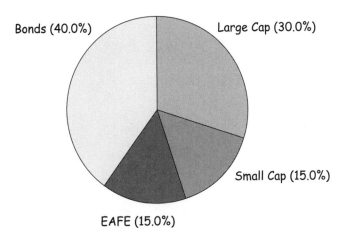

Bonds (40.0%)

Large Cap (30.0%)

Small Cap (15.0%)

EAFE (15.0%)

Target 5-year growth rate: 8–10%

Total rate of return since 1970: 12.2%

Beta: 0.65

Average of four worst quarters: –8.9%

Average of four worst years: –12%

NOTES: _____

_____

_____

_____

_____

PORTFOLIO 3—GROWTH

RISKOMETER

EXHIBIT 3-5c

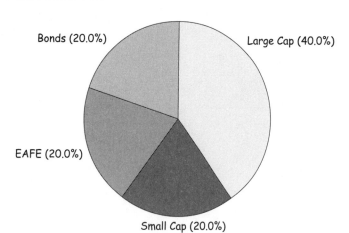

Bonds (20.0%)

Large Cap (40.0%)

EAFE (20.0%)

Small Cap (20.0%)

Target 5-year growth rate: 9–11%

Total rate of return since 1970: 13.2%

Beta: 0.82

Average of four worst quarters: –12.22%

Average of four worst years: –16.3%

NOTES: _____

_____

_____

_____

_____

_____

PORTFOLIO 4—AGGRESSIVE

EXHIBIT 3-5d

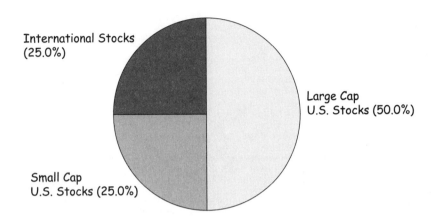

Target 5-year growth rate: 11–13%

Total rate of return since 1970: 14.2%

Beta: 0.99

Average of four worst quarters: –15.6%

Average of four worst years: –20%

The U.S. large cap and small cap should be equally weighted between growth and value.

NOTES: _____

_____

_____

_____

_____

If you want to compare these four portfolios with how the S&P Index has done in the period since 1970, here are the statistics (see Exhibit 3-6):

S&P Index:

Total rate of return since 1970: 13.9%

Beta: 1.00

Average of four worst quarters: –18%

Average of four worst years: –16.2%

EXHIBIT 3-6 Individual Asset Classes Since 1970

	Rate of Return, %	Beta	Average of Worst Four Quarters, %	Average of Worst Four Years, %
Large-Cap Growth	12.9	1.13	–29.7	–29.7
Large-Cap Value	15.6	0.83	–17.6	–10.9
Small-Cap Growth	8.97	1.4	–29.5	–28.8
Small-Cap Value	17.6	1.1	–23.2	–18.4
EAFE	13.2	0.75	–19.5	–17.8
Long-Term Gov. Bonds	8.94	0.25	–10.3	–5.8
Short-Term Gov. Bonds	7.78	0.0	–0.4	3.8

If you notice that your level of decline tolerance exceeds the average of the worst four quarters, please remember that we're not taking a snapshot of what happened through the quarter, and that certainly there were periods where you were down a lot more in the course of the quarter than the number you see above.

NOTES: _____

_____

_____

_____

 Go to your IPS on pages 7–9 and write in which portfolios or asset classes are appropriate for each time horizon in question 8.

Congratulations! This IPS is now your investment road map allowing you to take full responsibility for your own investment portfolio decisions. You now have the choice of going it alone or hiring an investment advisor.

SHOULD YOU DO IT YOURSELF OR WORK WITH AN ADVISOR?

You probably will not need to work with an advisor on your short-term money because it's cash, CDs, or money market accounts, and you can do that yourself. The fewer the people involved at this stage, the higher your return will be. If you want to capture some significant growth with your mid-term money, you might want to work with an advisor. Your long-term money is the place where an advisor can make the most difference.

Reasons you should consider working with an advisor are:

- To free up your time and get professional implementation
- To get professional, ongoing supervision
- To become aware of any important changes that might occur in the financial services industry and determine whether they should be included in your portfolios

The investment policy statement also creates a measuring benchmark to review investment portfolio performance. If goals and objectives have been clearly defined, it becomes much easier to determine how the portfolio is performing relative to those goals and objectives.

Understand that if you want an advisor to help you, you will have to pay for it. Cheaper is not necessarily better. As with any profession, like lawyers or doctors, the more you have at risk the more you will spend on quality advice.

The Cost of Advice

Advisors come in many types. The most important thing you need to be aware of is that for advisors to make money, clients must have a certain level of assets. To get quality advice, you're typically going to need a minimum of $50,000 of investable dollars. If you have less than that, the advisor is going to have to charge very high fees as a percentage of your total assets. Obviously, the more money you have, the more cost efficient your portfolio will be. Typically, investors with $100,000 or more will pay around 2 percent a year to implement an investment strategy, of which 1 percent goes to the advisor and 1 percent goes to the money manager. There are usually additional expenses (such as built-in mutual fund expenses) that can add up to the average client spending around 3 percent a year for their portfolio to be actively managed. When your portfolio grows above $250,000, your fees typically drop by about 50 to 100 basis points and you can also receive a higher level of customized advice.

Is this too high a cost? Only if you would do better, after fees, by yourself. It is important to remember when you pay for a service, that the cost is not as important as the after-cost results—and whatever your alternative might be.

What the Advisor Does to Earn His or Her Fee. A good advisor will look at your IPS and work with you to decide the most efficient way to accomplish what you need to get done. For example, is a mutual fund the right answer? Is an active or a passive fund right for you? Is a separate account the right answer or are individual stocks the right answer? Advisors typically are specialists in two key areas: how to implement your allocation strategy, and which investment vehicles might be best suited to you.

Many advisors do not actually manage money themselves. They are like a general practitioner in the business of understanding you and then finding specialists for each area of your portfolio.

What Kind of Investor Are You? Your personality type will determine what type of advisor is best for you. What personality type did you mark in Section One?

- Adventurer
- Individualist
- Celebrity
- Guardian
- Straight-Arrow

Typically, the guardian and the celebrity benefit the most by working with an advisor. Adventurers and individualists who do not enjoy investing would benefit in the sense that they can shift their time and energy to other things. However, some adventurers and individualists really enjoy doing the investing and do not work very well with advisors because they end up questioning their decisions.

Which are you? _____

_____

QUESTIONS TO ASK AN ADVISOR

As part of deciding who to work with, you should ask the following questions:

1. What is the advisor's educational background, and does he or she have any certifications from independent associations? (Having a college degree doesn't qualify someone for investment consulting.)

2. What percentage of clients is fee-based? Sixty to 70 percent or more is favorable. Or, how does he or she get paid?

3. What investment vehicles are offered: mutual funds, individually managed accounts, and/or annuities?

4. Ask about the advisor's own investment history. Is the advisor doing what he or she is advising you to do?

5. Why have they lost clients in the past? The real question is did they learn something from the experience?

6. And one of the most important questions that people rarely ask, "Can you provide three references?" Fee-based advisors generally don't mind at all if you ask for references from existing clients.

Whether you choose to work with an advisor, we recommend that you complete the rest of Section Three to get some idea of the kind of investing you should do. You can use this workbook as a reference to look up investments that an advisor selects for you. This way, you're not just blindly handing your money to somebody to manage it; you have enough information to know if what an advisor suggests makes sense for your situation. If an advisor tells you they can get you a 20 percent return, or wants to put your serious money into gold futures, you may want to quietly get up and dismiss yourself from the table.

Also, if the advisor chooses a strategy that doesn't fit with your investment personality, you can request that he or she changes it to one that suits you better. The highest probability of success comes from:

- Knowing your risk tolerance
- Understanding the different investments
- Having a strategy that works, and one that fits with your own personal temperament

SELECTING A FINANCIAL ADVISOR

Sometimes even the most independent of us needs professional help to work out a particularly tough investment problem. We'll show you how to decide when you need a pro—and how to find the right one.

In this section we provide a list of the different types of financial advisors, a description of what each type does, and how they get paid.

Hiring an advisor doesn't mean you must give up all control. The exact role an advisor plays in your individual investment arena is up to you. You may opt for an advisor who analyzes your financial condition, strategizes with you on the best route forward, then sends you on your way—in other words, someone who empowers you to take action on your own. The more hands-on help you want, the more it will cost, but an ongoing relationship may be worth it.

If you work with an advisor, here are the things to look for:

Reputation: How many accounts does the firm have and how many have been brought in over the last five years? How many have been lost? How big is the firm, both in terms of people and in assets under management? Bigger is not necessarily better.

Investment Strategy: Does the advisor have a well-defined, consistently applied investment process? What are the advisor's primary sources of research? Who participates in the investment decisions? How are tax considerations factored into the investment process?

Account Management: How does the advisor rate in client service?

The Financial Advisor Community

Think of the variety of professionals selling investments and advice as different divisions of the armed services. The Army, Navy, Marine Corps, and Air Force all have a similar objective and often use the same type of equipment; they just carry out their missions differently.

Many investors assume their brokers are well-trained money managers. This is not necessarily true. Anyone who can pass one six-hour test administered by the National Association of Securities dealers can become a broker. Full-service broker-dealers have relationships with a universe of money managers and large research departments.

Stockbrokers believe they're at the top of the pecking order; bank representatives believe they sell on hallowed ground; and fee-only advisors sense they are close to nirvana. Yet they all may be selling the same exact investment product or offering the same service. Their joint mission is to help their clients successfully meet their financial goals. Unfortunately, financial advisors with the highest marks and those with the worst records are all known by the same title. The public can't tell who is competent and who is not, so how does an investor choose?

Let's take a closer look at your choices:

Financial Planners. This group can be either advisors or brokers, depending on whether they specialize in financial planning, and can charge fees for services and/or commissions. They can provide you with for-fee or free financial planning reports which can cost hundreds, or thousands, of dollars elsewhere.

For a fee, consultants in many large firms can help you establish your investment objectives, do the research and due diligence needed to find an appropriate money manager for you, and—most important—provide sophisticated monitoring and review of the money manager who is managing your account.

You still need to be aware that more than 200,000 women and men call themselves financial planners, including accountants, attorneys, stockbrokers, insurance agents, self-styled money managers, credit counselors, and the Internet junkie down the street. But only a small number of these are registered certified financial planners, a designation that guarantees a person has passed a rigorous set of tests in all areas of personal finance (investing, retirement and estate planning, taxes, insurance, and more), and has at least three years of experience in the field.

- **Certified Financial Planner**. To earn this designation, candidates must pass a comprehensive, 10-hour examination given by the Denver-based Certified Financial Planner Board of Standards. Every two years after receiving their degrees, CFPs must complete 30 hours of continuing education to remain certified. Most CFPs are self-employed. Others are brokers, accountants, lawyers, or insurance agents. Some are fee-only, meaning they charge a set fee for advice or to develop a plan. Others also charge commissions for selling products.

- **Chartered Financial Consultant**. ChFCs offer comprehensive financial planning services. They must take 10 courses on financial planning topics and pass 10 two-hour exams prepared by The American College in Bryn Mawr, PA. ChFCs must also complete 60 hours of continuing education every two years. Typically, they charge a flat fee for developing a financial plan.

- **Certified Public Accountant/Personal Financial Specialist (CPA/PFS)**. Designated by the American Institute of Certified Public Accountants, based in New York, a CPA must pass an exam and meet work-experience requirements. A PFS must pass a comprehensive exam given by the American Institute of Certified Public Accountants and perform a designated number of hours of personal financial planning services and continuing education.

- **Chartered Financial Analyst**. A CFA is viewed as the most prestigious credential in the investment industry; however, the credential focuses on investment analysis rather than financial planning. Most CFAs specialize in securities analysis and provide investment advice. Many are personal money managers. Others manage portfolios for mutual funds, trust companies, or broker-dealers. CFA candidates must pass three exams over a minimum of three years administered by AIMR, the Association of Investment Management and Research in Charlottesville, VA. Many portfolio managers who manage separate accounts are CFAs.

- **Registered Investment Advisors**. RIAs must file an informational form (Form ADV) with the SEC annually and pay a one-time fee. It is important to note that the designation RIA does not necessarily mean that the person is qualified to manage your money. By law, these advisors must give you Part II of the Form ADV, which covers fee structure, financial services, and investment strategy. But you also need Part I, and the accompanying schedules, which detail disciplinary actions, education, account custody arrangements, and the number of clients the advisor counsels.

Full-Service Brokers. Most full-service stockbrokers solicit business and are paid by commissions. Full-service means they offer a wider variety of financial products than discount brokerages and charge considerably higher fees. Products they offer include stocks, bonds, derivatives, annuities, and insurance. They also offer investment advice and research.

Many stockbrokers attempt to add value by following traditional investment strategies such as trying to pick exceptional securities, stocks, or mutual funds or predicting which way the market's going.

Active strategies entail investigation and analysis expenses, and these judgment calls also may involve the acceptance of a degree of diversifiable risk. The extra costs and risks can be substantial and must be justified by realistically evaluated return expectations. Ideally, your stockbroker is no longer going to be paid on a transaction basis. You're going to pay him or her a fee for advice, which ultimately means you're going to pay for results.

Discount Brokers. Discount brokerages usually don't offer the full range of services or research provided by full-service brokers. Most do not offer advice; they simply transact trades. Because they manage fewer products than their full-service counterparts, discounters charge considerably lower fees. Discounters also often offer online computer order entry services. Those that have live brokers generally pay them a set salary to execute trades. The brokers don't solicit and aren't paid commissions. Discount brokerages make money by doing business in volume, competing mostly on price and reliability of the service. If they have the lowest prices and the best service, they get the most trades.

Bank Investment Representatives. This is like having a "broker-in-the-bank." For decades, consumers have listed banks as the most trusted source of financial products and advice. The primary reason: bank savings and CDs are backed by the FDIC. Traditional bankers, however, knew little about investments, financial planning, or diversification; and bank employees were trained basically in making loans, taking deposits, and issuing credit cards. A few years ago, banks decided to cross over and offer investments through subsidiaries or affiliates, since banks are prohibited from offering investments directly. These bank affiliate advisors have the same securities licenses as other brokers, and many have gone through traditional Wall Street training programs.

Investment Management Consultants. Pure-investment management consultants normally work for Wall Street firms and specialize in consulting with investors about their investments. They help investors set financial goals and come up with comprehensive plans, rather than simply trying to sell particular investments. They charge fees for services rather than charging commissions on transactions.

They take a much broader approach and maintain a macro perspective of global, small-cap, and large-cap equities. They attend training sessions and carry professional designations:

- **IIMC.** Institute for Investment Management Consultants, based in Washington, DC and Phoenix.

- **Certified Investment Management Consultant (CIMC).** Designated by the IIMC to members who pass an exam and have at least three years of professional consulting financial experience.

- **Certified Investment Management Specialist (CIMS).** Designated by the IIMC to associate members who pass an exam and meet financial service work-experience requirements.

Independent Fee-Only Financial Advisors. There are various types of advisors, and many are very good. They act in ways that are similar to the big Wall Street firms' investment management consultants, and like investment management consultants, these advisors have no incentive to sell you a financial product for the commission they'll personally gain. They still have access to all the mutual fund vendors and meet with representatives of many mutual fund companies.

Look for financial advisors who have formed alliances with professionals in related fields; who have set up formalized networking relationships with existing planners, estate planners, CPAs, state attorneys, and/or insurance specialists; or who have become certified financial planners.

Where to Turn. These professional organizations will provide you with select lists of financial planners in your area.

- **American Institute of CPAs.** Lists CPA Personal Financial Specialists. Call 888-999-9256.
- **The Institute of Certified Financial Planners.** Lists financial planners with a CFP designation. Call 303-759-4900.
- **Licensed Independent Network of CPA Financial Planners (LINC).** Lists members who are CPSA/PFS fee-only planners in public accounting firms. Call 800-737-2727.

HOW DO ADVISORS GET PAID?

Different advisors charge differently. Some charge a commission; some charge a fee. Typically, you will be better off working with an advisor who charges a flat fee. While these considerations are important, far more important is what you get for what you pay. Some advisors charge the same fee as others but provide a lot less, so the real struggle is finding an advisor who will give you what you need and charge the right amount.

With smaller accounts, typically an advisor is going to charge you a commission. For those with under $50,000 to invest, it's important that you stay with your investments for the long-term since transaction expenses will cut into your portfolio's gains.

Most stockbrokers are paid commissions on mutual funds, such as 12b-1s, and dealer concessions. When you see a 12b-1 fee, it's generally paid annually, 15–35 basis points based on the assets. Dealer concessions generally are paid on the front end of all new assets the broker brings in, within a range of 25 basis points to 100 points. In the case of insurance bundled products, a stockbroker often can earn a higher rate. *Note:* Some wirehouse firms that pay front-ends typically have surrender fees attached if the client decides to move out of it. This discourages clients from leaving or switching firms.

Investment advisors do not have to share the revenue with anyone else when they charge for services. They typically charge an annual asset fee based on a graduated schedule. Ask if your investment advisor receives any other fees when working with a fund manager.

The services we're talking about cost about as much as buying a no-load mutual fund. For a $3 million portfolio, the firm's fees, plus what the average advisor charges, total about 1.6 percent.

Compensation from commissions clients pay on investments they purchase as a result of the advisor's advice sets up a potential conflict of interest and a proceed-with-caution sign for you. Since the advisor or planner will profit most from high-load and high-commission items, it's tempting to recommend those items to you, whether or not they really suit your pocketbook and goals. It's best to derail the profit motive and pay a set fee for a planner's advice.

Other Potential Concerns. Often new or unsophisticated financial advisors will gravitate toward their own firm's internal investment managers because the sales brochures are handy, the information flow is better, and the firm has a department to support. This is especially true if the outside money manager program is relatively new to the firm.

Our suggestion is to first find a good advisor, then let the advisor help you find a good money manager. A firm using outside money management firms often signs on to accounts as a fiduciary and helps with account processing. These are the people you want to hire.

Independence and objectivity are critical. Your advisor should be on your side, looking for the best solutions for you, even if those are managers or investment specialists outside of his or her own firm.

What You Need to Know to Pick an Advisor. It's still up to you to do your homework. At the end of the day, you really need to establish a list of criteria for your specific needs. Ask the appropriate questions, and if any answer is unacceptable, go on to the next advisor. The best way to find an advisor is by word of mouth.

Take your time. Don't be pressured, and try to find the right person, someone who you're comfortable with and who will be on your side.

LIST OF CRITERIA: _____

_____

_____

_____

If you have chosen to go with an advisor, begin interviewing and select the one you are most comfortable with who will help you to reach your goals as stated in your IPS on pages 7–9.

DOING IT YOURSELF

We recommend that if you're going to manage your own portfolio, you should use index funds to invest, and use a passive allocation strategy that will not tempt you to move in and out of the market.

Often investors don't realize how much *time* must be invested in managing their own portfolios. It involves accumulating and analyzing many specifics, such as a forecast for return for each of the investments in your portfolio, and understanding how the investments work together in terms of generating risk in that portfolio.

If you decide to implement the strategy yourself, you can go to an online broker (like Schwab, Fidelity, or CSFB) and buy yourself appropriate index funds—just go to stock funds in each of the appropriate asset classes (Exhibit 3-7). Buy them and put them in that block.

EXHIBIT 3-7 Firms Offering Funds and Advice

Fund Name	Investment Objective	Fund Family	Phone
Advance Capital I Bond	Corp Hi Qlty	Advance Capital I Group	800-345-4783
American Gas Index	Sp. Nat. Res.	Rushmore Group	800-343-3355
ASM	Growth-Inc	ASM Fund	800-445-2763
Benham Gold Equities Index	Sp. Metals	Benham Group	800-331-8331
Biltmore Equity Index	Growth-Inc	Biltmore Funds	800-462-7538
BT Investment Equity 500 Idx	Growth	BT Funds	800-943-2222
California Invmt S&P 500 Idx	Growth-Inc	California Investment Trust Group	800-225-8778
California Invmt S&P MidCap	Growth	California Investment Trust Group	800-225-8778
Capital Market Index	Growth-Inc	Capital Market Fund	800-328-7408
Colonial Small Stock A	Small Company	Colonial Group	800-248-2828
Composite Northwest 50 A	Growth	Composite Group of Funds	800-543-8072
Dean Witter Value-Add Mkt Eq	Growth-Inc	Dean Witter Funds	800-869-3863
Domini Social Equity	Growth-Inc	Domini Social Equity Trust	800-762-6814
Dreyfus Edison Electric	Sp. Util	Dreyfus Group	800-645-6561
Dreyfus-Wilshire Lrg Co Grth	Growth	Dreyfus Group	800-645-6561
Dreyfus-Wilshire Lrg Co Val	Growth	Dreyfus Group	800-645-6561
Dreyfus-Wilshire Sm Co Grth	Small Company	Dreyfus Group	800-645-6561
Dreyfus-Wilshire Sm Co Value	Small Company	Dreyfus Group	800-645-6561
Fidelity Market Index	Growth-Inc	Fidelity Group	800-544-8888
First American Equity Indx A	Growth-Inc	First American Investment Funds	800-637-2548
First American Equity Indx B	Growth	First American Investment Funds	800-637-2548
Galaxy II Large Company Indx	Growth-Inc	Galaxy Funds	800-628-0414
Galaxy II Small Company Indx	Small Company	Galaxy Funds	800-628-0414
Galaxy II U.S. Treasury Indx	Gvt Treasury	Galaxy Funds	800-628-0414
Galaxy II Utility Index	Sp. Util	Galaxy Funds	800-628-0414
Gateway Index Plus	Growth-Inc	Gateway Group	800-354-6339
Gateway Mid-Cap Index	Growth	Gateway Group	800-354-6339
Gateway Small Cap Index	Small Company	Gateway Group	800-354-6339

EXHIBIT 3-7 Firms Offering Funds and Advice (*Continued*)

Jackson National Growth	Growth	Jackson National Capital Mgmt Funds	800-888-3863
MainStay Equity Index	Growth-Inc	MainStay Funds	800-522-4202
Monitrend Summation	Growth-Inc	Monitrend Mutual Funds	800-251-1970
Nations Equity-Index Tr A	Growth	Nations Funds	800-321-7854
Peoples Index	Growth-Inc	Dreyfus Group	800-645-6561
Peoples S&P MidCap Index	Growth	Dreyfus Group	800-645-6561
Portico Bond Immdex	Corp Hi Qlty	Portico Funds	800-228-1024
Portico Equity Index	Growth-Inc	Portico Funds	800-228-1024
Principal Pres S&P 100 Plus	Growth-Inc	Principal Preservation Portfolios	800-826-4600
Schwab 1000	Growth-Inc	Schwab Funds	800-526-8600
Schwab International Index	Foreign	Schwab Funds	800-526-8600
Schwab Small Cap Index	Small Company	Schwab Funds	800-526-8600
Seven Seas Matrix Equity	Growth	Seven Seas Series Fund	617-654-6089
Seven Seas S&P 500 Index	Growth-Inc	Seven Seas Series Fund	617-654-6089
Seven Seas S&P Midcap Index	Growth	Seven Seas Series Fund	617-654-6089
Smith Breeden Mkt Tracking	Growth-Inc	Smith Breeden Family of Funds	800-221-3138
Stagecoach Corporate Stock	Growth-Inc	Stagecoach Funds	800-222-8222
STI Classic Intl Eqty IdxInv	Foreign	STI Classic Funds	800-428-6970
T. Rowe Price Equity Index	Growth-Inc	Price T. Rowe Funds	800-638-5660
U.S. Large Stock	Growth-Inc	U.S. Large Stock	800-366-7266
United Svcs All American Eq	Growth-Inc	United Services Funds	800-873-8637
Vanguard Balanced Index	Balanced	Vanguard Group	800-662-7447
Vanguard Bond Indx Long-Term	Corp General	Vanguard Group	800-662-7447
Vanguard Bond Indx Short-Trm	Corp General	Vanguard Group	800-662-7447
Vanguard Bond Indx Total Bd	Corp Hi Qlty	Vanguard Group	800-662-7447
Vanguard Index 500	Growth-Inc	Vanguard Group	800-662-7447
Vanguard Index Extended Mkt	Small Company	Vanguard Group	800-662-7447
Vanguard Index Growth	Growth	Vanguard Group	800-662-7447
Vanguard Index Small Cap Stk	Small Company	Vanguard Group	800-662-7447
Vanguard Index Total Stk Mkt	Growth-Inc	Vanguard Group	800-662-7447
Vanguard Index Value	Growth-Inc	Vanguard Group	800-662-7447
Vanguard Intl Eqty Emerg Mkt	Foreign	Vanguard Group	800-662-7447
Vanguard Intl Eqty European	Europe	Vanguard Group	800-662-7447
Vanguard Intl Eqty Pacific	Pacific	Vanguard Group	800-662-7447
Vanguard Quantitative	Growth-Inc	Vanguard Group	800-662-7447
Victory Stock Index	Growth-Inc	Victory Group	800-539-3863
Woodward Equity Index Ret	Growth-Inc	Woodward Funds	800-688-3350

It is important to realize that it is not enough just to implement the strategy; you must make sure that the vehicles you invest in are operating the way you want them to. There are some tasks that need to be done.

Things You Should Know Before You Start
Buying and Selling on Your Own

Mutual fund managers trade shares of stock on the stock exchanges where member brokers (agents) buy and sell stocks and bonds of American and foreign businesses on behalf of the public. A stock exchange provides a marketplace for stocks and bonds in the same way a commodity exchange does for commodities.

To most investors, "the stock market" means the New York Stock Exchange, which has been in existence for more than 200 years. The New York Stock Exchange (NYSE) is an agency auction market. What does that really mean and what are the advantages? The essential point is that trading at the NYSE takes place by open bids and offers by Exchange members, acting as agents for institutions or individual investors. Buy and sell orders meet directly on the trading floor, and prices are determined by the interplay of supply and demand. In contrast, in the over-the-counter market, the price is determined by a dealer who buys and sells out of inventory.

At the NYSE, each listed stock is assigned to a single post where the specialist manages the auction process. NYSE members bring all orders for NYSE-listed stocks to the Exchange floor either electronically or by a floor broker. As a result, the flow of buy and sell orders for each stock is funneled to a single location.

This heavy stream of diverse orders provides liquidity—the ease with which securities can be bought and sold without wide price fluctuations.

The Trading Floor is still where all NYSE transactions occur. It is a 36,000-square-foot facility designed specifically to support the centralized auction. It is where market professionals, supported by advanced technology, represent the orders of buyers and sellers to determine prices according to the laws of supply and demand.

The Trading Floor houses the market maker trading posts, each peopled by specialists and specialist clerks. Every listed security is traded in a unique location at one of these posts and by one specialist, thus ensuring that each trading interest is centralized. All buying and selling takes place around these posts.

After an order has been completed in the auction market, a report of execution is returned directly to the member firm office over the same electronic circuit that brought the order to the Trading Floor.

How a Stock Exchange Operates. Stocks handled by one or more stock exchanges are called *listed stocks*. A company that wants to have its stock listed for trading on an exchange must first prove to the exchange that it has enough paid-up capital, is a lawful enterprise, and is in good financial condition.

How Stocks Trade on the Exchange. Probably one of the most confusing aspects of investing is understanding how stocks actually trade. Words like *bid, ask, volume,* and *spread* can be quite confusing if you do not understand what they mean. Depending on which exchange a stock trades, there are two different systems.

The New York Stock Exchange and the American Stock Exchange (composed of the Boston, Philadelphia, Chicago, and San Francisco exchanges) are both listed exchanges, meaning that brokerage firms contribute individuals known as *specialists* who are responsible for all of the trading in a specific stock. This is known as *an open auction market*. Volume, or the number of shares that trade on a given day, is counted by the specialists.

Specialists control stock prices by matching buy and sell orders delivered by the floor brokers shouting out their orders. The specialists change the prices to match the supply-and-demand fundamentals. The specialist system was created to guarantee that every seller finds a buyer, and vice versa. This process may sound chaotic, but specialists do succeed in their function of maintaining an orderly market and matching sellers to buyers.

Sample Order Execution

1. Enter an order through your online broker.

2. Your broker either electronically sends the order to a specialist operating on the exchange floor or routes it to a floor broker at the exchange, who physically walks the order over to the trading area.

3. The market specialist consolidates your order with all others, then announces the best available price as well as the number of shares available at that price.

4. The floor broker makes a bid for the stock based on that price, competing with other brokers assembled in the trading area.

5. The specialist awards the stock to successful bidders. If no buyers appear, the specialist is required by the NYSE to be buyer of last resort. In exchange for providing liquidity in the stock, the specialist is allowed to profit from the price differential of stocks he or she buys during price declines, then sells as the price rises.

Over-the-Counter (OTC) Market. Investors also trade on the OTC market. The stock market, the SmallCap, and the OTC Bulletin Board are the three main over-the-counter markets. In an over-the-counter market, brokerages, also known as broker-dealers, act as market makers for various stocks. The brokerages interact over a centralized computer system, providing liquidity for the market to function. One firm represents the seller and offers an ask price (also called the *offer*), or the price the seller is asking to sell the security. Another firm represents the buyer and gives a bid, or a price at which the buyer will buy the security.

For example, a particular stock might be trading at a bid of $10 and an ask of $10.50. If an investor wanted to sell shares, she would get the bid price of $10 per share; if she wanted to buy shares, she would pay the ask price of

$10.50 per share. The difference is called the *spread*, which is paid by the buyer. This difference is split between the two firms involved in the transaction. Volume on over-the-counter markets is often double-counted, as both the buying firm and the selling firm report their activity.

Unlike the NYSE, the NASDAQ is not a physical exchange, but rather, composed of a network of thousands of dealers who are connected electronically. Sometimes called the *screen based market*, the market relies on individual market makers rather than a single specialist to provide liquidity in over-the-counter securities. These market makers combine their efforts in each stock to collectively provide a market. This is referred to as honoring the two-sided market.

Online Stock Investing. Just a few years ago, online stock trading was nothing more than cyber curiosity; now it has exploded into popularity. Online investing articles fill magazines and make the headlines of every major newspaper's front page. In 1999, the number of Americans investing over the Internet grew 120 percent. Online trading accounts for every seventh retail stock trade. It is estimated that there are more than seven million online investing accounts, representing 20 percent of all brokerage accounts, and that percentage is expected to double.

Twelve online brokers, combined, control 90 percent of all online brokerage accounts: Ameritrade, Charles Schwab, Datek Online, Discover Brokerage Direct, DLJ Direct, E*Trade, Fidelity, National Discount Brokers, Quick & Reilly, SureTrade, Waterhouse, and Web Street Securities. While these brokers are popular with the public and are featured in the media in price comparison charts, they are not necessarily popular trading sites.

While it's true the new direct trading systems bypass profit-taking middlemen, namely the specialists and market makers who work behind the scenes, if you don't already understand how the various markets work, you won't understand the services the different sites offer, the order entry or execution process, or the reason they charge what they do.

Electronic Communication Networks (ECNs) give traders the ability to bypass a market maker and buy and sell directly with other traders. ECNs work as order matching systems, and allow traders to advertise a price sometimes better than the current bid or offer. If there is no match for your order on the system, it is posted electronically on the Level II screen, which is virtually the same as having access to the Level III market maker's screen. In fact, your order is seen by every Level II screen in the world. Some of the larger ECNs are:

Archipelago (TNTO)   Terra Nova and Townsend Analytics smart ECN
InstiNet (INCA)   Reuters system for institutions

Island (ISLD)	Datek Trading
(BTRD)	Bloomberg's Trade Book
RediBook (REDI)	Spear Leeds

There are about 10 major ECNs which quite often are quoting better prices than the NASDAQ. The granddaddy of the ECNs is InstiNet (INCA). InstiNet is a system set up to allow big institutions to bargain with each other. InstiNet allows a mechanism for two institutional investors to come together on a price anonymously. While you pay a premium for using an ECN, the price improvement that you get on a thousand shares more than offsets that premium.

Don't Quit Your Day Job:

- *Don't mix up the term* day trading *with investing. Day trading is highly speculative.*
- *A recent SEC examination has interesting findings.*
- *Day traders need to be well funded and incredibly good to survive.*

Day traders engage in the practice of riding the stock market's ups and downs, trying to squeeze profits by rapidly buying and selling shares. There are many firms around the country set up to service individuals desiring to get in on the activity.

A 1999 SEC examination of 67 day-trading firms had some fascinating findings. The study found that a trader making a fairly average 50 trades a day, and paying the modest commission structure of a flat $16.70 per trade, spends $16,700 a month in trading expenses (50 × $16.70 × 20). Add to that $150 a month in data feeds, and he or she would have to generate a staggering $202,000 a year in profits to simply cover expenses.

This does not include the impact of taxes (almost all gains are short-term in nature) or the cost of margin borrowing, in which many traders engage. A trader starting with a million dollars of assets would need to capture in excess of 20 percent a year simply to break even (assuming no taxes and no loans to cover margin requirements). Considering that very few managers outperform the market, and that the long-term return for stocks is anywhere from 11 to 15 percent, depending on the time period, the day trader needs to be incredibly good to survive.

The end result? A Senate subcommittee found that 80 percent of day traders lost money. Another study by Washington State found that 77 percent of day traders lose money. We're not sure about the internal rate of return (IRR) for the remaining 20 percent, but we are sure that most day traders would be better off working with a professional to manage their serious money, and spending their time on more lucrative ventures.

Day trading is something most first time investors should avoid. Only after an investor has gained a great deal of knowledge about, and confidence in, his or her abilities, should day trading be considered. Additionally, day trading fits only those investors with certain risk-reward parameters. Check your IPS and your personality type before deciding whether day trading might be an option for you.

NOTES: _____

_____

_____

_____

_____

CONCLUSION

There we are, we're done. We've tried to cut through the noise and make investing concepts as easy to understand as possible. Some parts of this book were very difficult to write without getting into complicated math and deeper explanations, but our intention was to expose you to new concepts and to help you realize that you can win at the investing game.

 Did we answer the four most important challenges that every first time investor must address?

1. Do you understand your investment temperament? Yes!

2. Have we designed a successful portfolio that works for you? Yes!

3. Is your investment life manageable? Yes!

4. Do you have a plan to stay on the right course? Yes!

We've covered the basics of being a first time investor, but really we've taken you to a much higher level. We hope you will use the steps we've showed you to build a plan that meets your short-, mid-, and long-term investing goals.

GLOSSARY

Advisor: One who gives investment advice in return for compensation.

Aggressive growth: High risk/reward investments, funds, or securities classes.

Analysis: Process of evaluating individual financial instruments (often stock) to determine whether they are an appropriate purchase.

Analysts: Those on Wall Street who study and recommend securities.

Annual interest income: The annual dollar income for a bond or savings account calculated by multiplying the bond's coupon rate by its face value.

Annuity: A contract between an insurer and recipient (annuitant) whereby the insurer guarantees to pay the recipient a stream of income in exchange for premium payment(s).

Annuity beneficiary: Similar to the beneficiary of a life insurance policy, the annuity contract beneficiary receives a death benefit when another party to the annuity contract dies prior to the date on which the annuity begins paying out benefits.

Asset allocation: The decision as to how a person should be invested among major asset classes in order to increase expected risk-adjusted return. Asset allocation may be two-way (stocks and bonds), three-way (stocks, bonds, and cash), or many-way (i.e., value mutual funds, growth mutual funds, small mutual funds, cash, foreign mutual funds, foreign bonds, real estate, and venture capital).

Asset class: Assets composed of financial instruments with similar characteristics.

Asset-class investing: The disciplined purchase of groups of securities with similar risk/reward profiles.

Asset mix: Investable asset classes within a portfolio.

Average daily trading: The number of shares of stock traded in the preceding calendar month, multiplied by the current price and divided by 20 trading days.

Average return: The measure of the price of an asset, along with its income or yield on average over a specific time period. The arithmetic mean is the simple average of the returns in a series. The arithmetic mean is the appropriate measure of typical performance for a single period.

Back-end load: A fee charged at redemption by a mutual fund or a variable annuity to a buyer of shares.

Balanced index: A market index that serves as a basis of comparison for balanced portfolios. The balanced index is comprised of a 60 percent weighting of the S&P 500 Index and a 40 percent weighting of the SLH Government/ Corporate Bond Index. The balanced index relates unmanaged market returns to a balanced portfolio more precisely than either a stock or a bond index would alone.

Balanced mutual fund: A fund that includes two or more asset classes other than cash. In a typical balanced mutual fund, the asset classes are equities and fixed income securities. This term can be applied to any kind of portfolio that uses fixed income (bonds) as well as equity securities to reach goals. Many "boutique" investment managers are balanced managers, because it permits them to tailor the securities in a portfolio to the specific clients' cash flow needs and objectives. Balanced portfolios are often used by major mutual funds. They provide great flexibility.

Basis point: One basis point is 1/100th of a percentage point, or 0.01 percent. Basis points are often used to express changes or differences in yields, returns, or interest rates.

Bear market: A prolonged period of falling stock prices, typically exceeding 20 percent.

Beginning value: The market value of a portfolio at the inception of the period being measured by the customer statement.

Benchmark: A standard by which investment performance or trading execution can be judged. The most widely used performance benchmark is the total return of the S&P 500.

Beta: The linear relationship between the return on the security and the return on the market. By definition, the market, usually measured by the S&P 500 Index, has a beta of 1.00. Any stock or portfolio with a higher beta is generally more volatile than the market, while any with a lower beta is generally less volatile than the market.

Bond rating: Method of evaluating the possibility of default by a bond issuer. Standard & Poor's, Moody's Investors Service, and Fitch's Investors Service analyze the financial strength of each bond's issuer, whether a corporation or a government body. Their ratings range from AAA (highly unlikely to default) to D (in default). Bonds rated B or below are not investment grade—in other words, institutions that invest other people's money may not under most state laws buy them.

Bonds: Long-term, short-term, and high-yield. Debt instruments that pay lenders a regular return. Short-term bonds are five years or less. High-yield bonds pay lenders a higher rate of return because of higher risk.

Book-to-market ratio: Size of company's book (net) value relative to the market price of the company.

Broker: An individual with a series 7 license entitled to buy and sell securities, especially stock, on behalf of clients and charge for that service.

Broker-dealer: A firm employing brokers among other financial professionals.

Bull market: A prolonged period of rising stock prices. Typically an advance of greater than 30 percent.

Business day: A day when the New York Stock Exchange is open for trading.

Call option: A call option gives the investor the right, but not an obligation, to buy a security at a preset price within a specified time. A put gives the investor the right to sell a security at a preset price within a specified time. Calls and puts are therefore essentially bets on whether the underlying security will rise or fall in price. The option holders gain or lose in proportion to changes in the values of the new indexes, which in turn reflect the net asset value performances of the funds that comprise the indexes.

Cap: Stands for capitalization, as in small-cap, large-cap. The stock market worth of an individual equity. Large-cap stocks can be found on the New York Stock Exchange and the NASDAQ. Small-cap stocks are often listed on the NASDAQ.

Capital appreciation or depreciation: An increase or decrease in the value of a mutual fund or stock due to a change in the market price of the fund. For example, a stock that rises from $50 to $55 has capital appreciation of 10 percent. Dividends are not included in appreciation. If the price of the stock fell to $45, it would have depreciation of 10 percent.

Capital preservation: Investing in a conservative manner so as not to put capital at risk.

Cash: Investment in any instrument (often short-term) that is easily liquidated.

Commission: A transaction charge commonly levied by brokers and other financial middlemen for buying or selling securities.

Compound annual return: Geometric mean is another expression for compound annual return. The geometric mean is more appropriate when one is comparing the growth rate for an investment that is continually compounding.

Compounding: The reinvestment of dividends and/or interest and capital gains. This means that over time dividends and interest and capital gains grow exponentially; for example, a $100 earning compound interest at 10 percent a year would accumulate to $110 at the end of the first year and $121 at the end of the second year, and so on, based on the formula: compound sum = principal (1 + interest rate) number of periods.

Conservative: This is a characteristic relating to a mutual fund, a stock, or an investment style. There is no precise definition of the term. Generally, the term is used when the mutual fund manager's emphasis is on below-market betas.

Contrarian: An investment approach characterized by buying securities that are out of favor.

Core savings strategy: The home of your safe dollars that provides you overall financial security. A long-term commitment of savings not to be touched except in an emergency.

Correction: A correction is a reversal in the price of a stock, or the stock market as a whole, within a larger trend. While corrections most often are thought of as declines within an overall market rise, a correction also can be a temporary rise in the midst of a longer-term decline.

Correlation: A statistical measure of the degree to which the movement of two variables is related.

Coupon: The periodic interest payment on a bond. When expressed as an annual percentage, it is called the coupon rate. When multiplied by the face value of the bond, the coupon rate gives the annual interest income.

CPI: Consumer Price Index. Maintained by the Federal Bureau of Labor Statistics, it measures the changes in the cost of a specified group of consumer products relative to a base period. Because it represents the rate of inflation, the CPI can be used as a general benchmark for gauging the maintenance of purchasing power.

Currency risk: Possibility that foreign currency one holds may fall in value relative to investor's home currency, thus devaluing overseas investments.

Current return on equity (ROE): A ratio that measures profitability as the return on common stockholders' equity. It is calculated by dividing the reported earnings per share for the latest 12-month period by the book value per share.

Current yield: This is a bond's annual interest payment as a percentage of its current market price. The current yield is calculated by dividing the annual coupon interest for a bond by the current market price. The coupon rate and the current yield on a bond are equal when the bond is selling at par. Thus, a $1,000 bond with a coupon of 10 percent that is currently selling at $1,000 will have a current yield of 10.0 percent. However, if the bond's price drops to $800 the current yield becomes 12.5 percent.

$$\frac{\text{Annual coupon interest } (10\%)}{\$1,000.00} = 10\%$$

Deferred annuity: An annuity whose contract provides that payments to the annuitant be postponed until a number of periods have elapsed, for example, when the annuitant attains a certain age.

Deviation: Movement of instrument or asset class away from expected direction. In investment terminology most often associated with asset-class analysis.

Dissimilar price movement: The process whereby different asset classes and markets move in different directions.

Diversification: Spreading risk in one portfolio by putting assets in several categories of investments: stocks, bonds, and money market funds; several industries; or a mutual fund with a broad range of stocks.

Dividend: The payment from a company's earning normally paid on common shares declared by a company's board of directors to be distributed pro rata among the shares outstanding.

Dollar cost averaging: A system of buying stock or mutual funds at regular intervals with a fixed dollar amount. Under this system an investor buys by the dollar's worth rather than by the number of shares.

Dow Jones Industrial Average (DJIA): A price-weighted average of 30 leading blue chip industrial stocks, calculated by adding the prices of the 30 stocks and adjusting by a divisor, which reflects any stock dividends or splits. The Dow Jones Industrial Average is the most widely quoted index of the stock market, but it is not widely used as a benchmark for evaluating performance. The S&P 500 Index, which is more representative of the market, is the benchmark most widely used by performance measurement services.

Efficiency: The process of generating maximum reward from funds invested across a spectrum of asset classes.

Efficient frontier: The point where the maximum amount of risk an investor is willing to tolerate intersects with the maximum amount of reward that can potentially be generated.

Emerging growth mutual fund: Here, a mutual fund manager is looking for industries and companies whose growth rates are likely to be both rapid and independent of the overall stock market. "Emerging" means new. This implies such companies may be relatively small in size with the potential to grow much larger. Such stocks are generally much more volatile than the stock market in general and require constant, close attention to developments.

Emerging markets: Countries beginning to build financial marketplaces with appropriate safeguards.

EPS (earnings per share) growth: This is the annualized rate of growth in reported earnings per share of stock.

Equities: Stocks. Equity mutual funds are made up of many individual stocks. A stock is a right of ownership in a corporation.

Execution price: The negotiated price at which a security is purchased or sold.

Expected return: A tax term that means the expected amount to be received under an annuity contract, based on the periodic payment and the annuitant's life expectancy when the benefits begin.

Expenses: Cost of maintaining an invested portfolio.

Fee-based: A manager, advisor, or broker whose charges are based on a set amount rather than transaction charges.

Fee-only: A manager, advisor, or broker who charges an investor a preset amount for services.

Financial advisor/planner: One who helps investors with a wide variety of financial and investing issues including retirement, estate planning, and so forth. Often licensed and working for a larger financial entity.

Fixed annuities: The word "fixed" is used to describe the type of annuity referred to by the interest rate paid by the issuing insurance company on the fund's place in the annuity. The fixed annuity offers security in that the rate of return is certain. Typically, with a fixed annuity the insurance company declares a current interest rate and sets the interest rate.

Fixed income mutual funds: Mutual funds that invest in corporate bonds or government-insured mortgages, T-bills, Treasury bonds; if they own any stocks at all, these are usually preferred shares. They have a broad range of styles, involving market timing, swapping to gain quality or yield, setting up maturity ladders, and so on. A typical division of the fixed income market is between short (up to 3 years), intermediate (3 to 15 years), and long (15 to 30 years).

Forecasts: Predictions of analysts usually associated with stock picking and active money management.

401(k): Section of the Internal Revenue Code. In its most simple terms, a 401(k) plan is a before-tax employee savings plan.

Front-end load: A fee charged when an investor buys certain mutual funds or variable annuities.

Fund ratings: Evaluation of the performance of invested money pools, often mutual funds by such entities as Chicago-based Morningstar.

Fund shares: Shares in a mutual fund.

Fundamentals: This word refers to the financial statistics that traditional analysts and many valuation models use. Fundamental data include stock, earnings, dividends, assets and liabilities, inventories, debt, and so on. Fundamental data are in contrast to items used in technical analysis—such as price momentum, volume trends, and short sales statistics.

Global diversification: Investing funds around the world in regions and markets with dissimilar price movements.

Hot tip: Slang for an individual investment, often a stock, that is apparently poised to rise (but may not).

Income growth mutual fund: The primary purpose in security selection here is to achieve a current yield significantly higher than the S&P 500. The stability of the dividend and the rate of growth of the dividends is also of concern to the income buyer. These portfolios may own more utilities, less high tech, and may own convertible preferreds and convertible bonds.

Index fund: A passively managed portfolio designed and computer controlled to track the performance of a certain index, such as the S&P 500. In general, such mutual funds have performance within a few basis points of the target index. The most popular index mutual funds are those that track the S&P 500, but special index funds, such as those based on the Russell 1000 or the Wilshire 5000, also are available.

Indexing: Disciplined investing in a specific group (asset class) of securities designed to benefit from its aggregate performance.

Individual investor: Buyer or seller of securities for personal portfolio.

Investment objective: The financial goals one wishes to reach.

Inflation: A monetary phenomenon generated by an overexpansion of credit that drives up prices of assets while diminishing the worth of paper currency.

Institutional investor: Corporation or fund with market presence.

Interest: The rate a borrower pays a lender.

Intrinsic value: The theoretical valuation or price for a stock. The valuation is determined using a valuation theory or model. The resulting value is compared with the current market price. If the intrinsic value is greater than the market price, the stock is considered undervalued.

Invest: Disciplined process of placing money in financial instruments to gain a return. An individual who depends mostly on active management and stock-picking may be considered a speculator rather than investor.

Investment advisor: See planner, advisor.

Investment discipline: A specific money strategy one espouses.

Investment philosophy: Strategy justifying short- or long-term buying and selling of securities.

Investment policy statement (IPS): Embodies the essence of the financial planning process. It includes: assessing where you are now, detailing where you want to go, and developing a strategy to get there.

Investment wisdom: Process of understanding valid academic research concerning asset allocation.

Investor discomfort: Realization that risk is not appropriate and reward is not predictable in a given portfolio.

IPOs: Initial public offerings. The sale of stock in a company going public for the first time.

Liquidity: Ability to generate cash on demand when necessary.

Load funds: A mutual fund that is sold for a sales charge (load) by a brokerage firm or other sales representative. Such funds may be stock, bond, or commodity funds, with conservative or aggressive objectives. The stated advantage of a load fund is that the salesperson will explain the fund to the customer and advise him or her when it is appropriate to sell as well as when to buy more shares.

Lump-sum distribution: Single payment to a beneficiary covering the entire amount of an agreement. Participants in individual retirement accounts, pension plans, profit-sharing, and executive stock option plans generally can opt for a lump-sum distribution if the taxes are not too burdensome when they become eligible.

Management fee: Charge against investor assets for managing the portfolio of an open- or closed-end mutual fund as well as for such services as shareholder relations or administration. The fee, as disclosed in the prospectus, is a fixed percentage of the fund's asset value.

Margin: A loan often offered to investors by broker-dealers for the purpose of allowing the investor to purchase additional securities. In a down market, margin loans can be called and portfolios liquidated when the value of the loan threatens to exceed the value of the portfolio.

Market: In investing terms it is a place where securities are traded. Formerly a physical location, it may now refer to an electronic one as well.

Market bottom: The date that the bear leg of a market cycle reaches its low, not identified until some time after the fact. In the peak-to-peak cycle ended Sept. 30, 1987, the market bottom came on Aug. 12, 1982, when the S&P 500 closed at 102.42, down 27.1 percent from its previous bull market peak. The most recent bear leg ended on Dec. 4, 1987, when the S&P 500 closed at 223.9. Market bottoms can also be defined as the month- or quarter-end closest to the actual bottom date.

Market capitalization: The current value of a company determined by multiplying the latest available number of outstanding common shares by the current market price of a share. Market cap is also an indication of the trading liquidity of a particular issue.

Market timing: The attempt to base investment decisions on the expected direction of the market. If stocks are expected to decline, the timer may elect to hold a portion of the portfolio in cash equivalents or bonds. Timers may base their decisions on fundamentals (e.g., selling stocks when the market's price/book ratio reaches a certain level), on technical considerations (such as declining momentum or excessive investor optimism), or a combination of both.

Market value: The market or liquidation value of a given security or of an entire pool of assets.

Maturities: Applies to bonds. The date at which a borrower must redeem the capital portion of his or her loan.

Model portfolio: A theoretical construct of an investment or series of investments.

Modern Portfolio Theory: In 1950, Professor Harry Markowitz started to build an investment strategy that took more than 30 years to develop and be recognized as Modern Portfolio Theory; he won the Nobel Prize for his work in 1990.

Money market fund: Money market fund managers invest in short-term fixed instruments and cash equivalents. These instruments make up the portfolio and their objective is to maximize principal protection. Even though these accounts have short-term (one-day) liquidity, they typically pay more like 90- to 180-day CDs versus passbook or one-week CDs.

Municipal bonds: Fixed-income securities issued by governmental agencies.

Mutual fund: A pool of managed assets, regulated by the Securities and Exchange Commission, in which investors can purchase shares.

Mutual fund families: A mutual fund sponsor or company usually offers a number of funds with different investment objectives within its family of funds. For example, a mutual fund family may include a money market fund, a government bond fund, a corporate bond fund, a blue-chip stock fund, and a more speculative stock fund. If an investor buys a fund in the family, he or she is allowed to exchange that fund for another in the same family. This is usually done with no additional sales charge.

National Association of Securities Dealers, Inc. (NASD): The principal association of over-the-counter (OTC) brokers and dealers that establishes legal and ethical standards of conduct for its members. NASD was established in 1939 to regulate the OTC market in much the same manner as organized exchanges monitor actions of their members.

Net asset value (NAV): The market value of each share of a mutual fund. This figure is derived by taking a fund's total assets (securities, cash, and receivables), deducting liabilities, and then dividing that total by the number of shares outstanding.

Net trade: Generally, this is an over-the-counter trade involving no explicit commission. The investment advisor's compensation is in the spread between the cost of the security and the price paid by the customer. Also, a trade in which shares are exchanged directly with the issuer.

No-load funds: Mutual funds offered by an open-end investment company that imposes no sales charge (load) on its shareholders. Investors buy shares in no-load funds directly from the fund companies, rather than through a broker, as is done in load funds. Because no broker is used, no advice is given on when to buy or sell.

Nominal return: The actual current dollar growth in an asset's value over a given period. See also total return and real return.

Operating expenses: Cost associated with running a fund or portfolio.

Optimization: A process whereby a portfolio, invested using valid academic theory in various asset classes, is analyzed to insure that risk/reward parameters have not drifted from stated goals.

Outperform: Any given market that exceeds expectations or historical performance. Or, the term applied to a fund or portfolio manager whose performance is better than the market's.

Over-the-counter: A market made between securities dealers who act either as principal or broker for their clients. This is the principal markets for U.S. government and municipal bonds.

Percentage points: Used to describe the difference between two readings that are percentages. For example, if a portfolio's performance was 18.2 percent versus the S&P 500's 14.65, it outperformed the S&P by 3.6 percentage points.

Portfolio turnover: Removing funds from one financial instrument to place in another. This process can be costly due to fees, commissions, and taxes.

Price/earnings ratio (P/E): This may be defined as the current price dividend by reported earnings per share of stock for the latest 12-month period. For example, a stock with earnings per share during the trailing year of $5 and currently selling at $50 per share has a price/earnings ratio of 10.

Principal: The original dollar amount invested.

Prospectus: The document required by the Securities and Exchange Commission that accompanies the sale of a mutual fund or annuity outlining risks associated with certain types of funds or securities, fees and management. At the core of the prospectus is a description of the fund's investment objectives and the portfolio manager's philosophy.

Put: A put gives the investor the right, but not the obligation, to sell a security at a preset price within a specified time.

Quality growth mutual fund: This term implies long-term investment in high quality growth stocks, some of which might be larger, emerging companies while others might be long established household names. Such a portfolio might have volatility equal to or above that of the overall market, but less than that of an "emerging growth" portfolio.

Quartile: A ranking of comparative portfolio performance. The top 25 percent of mutual fund managers are in the first quartile, those ranking from the 26 percent to 50 percent are in the second quartile, from 51 percent to 75 percent in the third, and the lowest 25 percent in the fourth quartile.

Rate of return: The profits earned by a security as measured as a percentage of earned interest and/or dividends and/or appreciation.

Ratings: Performance and creditworthiness measurement of funds and corporations generated by Lipper, Moodys, Morningstar, and others. These ratings, when used to evaluate active fund managers, may be misleading since past performance is no guarantee of future success.

Real return: The inflation-adjusted return on an asset. Inflation-adjusted returns are calculated by subtracting the rate of inflation from an asset's apparent, or nominal, return. For example, if common stocks earn a total return of 10.3 percent over a period of time, but inflation during that period is 3.1 percent, the real return is the difference: 7.2 percent.

Rebalancing: A process whereby funds are shifted within asset classes and between asset class to insure the maintenance of the efficient frontier. See optimization.

Reinvested dividends: Dividends paid by a particular mutual fund that are reinvested in that same mutual fund. Some mutual funds offer automatic dividend reinvestment programs (DRIPs). In the complex equation theoretically used to determine the performance of the S&P 500, each company's dividend is reinvested in the stock of that company.

REITs: Real estate investment trusts: bundled, securitized real estate assets often trading on the New York Stock Exchange.

Relative return: The return of a stock or a mutual fund portfolio compared with some index, usually the S&P 500.

Risk: Risk is nothing more than the uncertainty of future rates of return, which includes the possibility of loss. This variability or uncertainty causes "rational" investors to expect higher returns on investments where the actual timing or amount of payoffs is not guaranteed.

Risk-free rate of return: The return on an asset that is considered virtually riskless. U.S. government Treasury bills are typically used as the risk-free asset because of their short time horizon and the low probability of default.

Risk tolerance: Investors' innate ability to deal with the potential of losing money without abandoning investment process.

ROI: Return on investment. The amount of money generated over time by placement of funds in specific financial instruments.

S&P 500: The performance benchmark most widely used by sponsors, managers, and performance measurement services. This index includes 400 industrial stocks, 20 transportation stocks, 40 financial stocks, and 40 public utilities. Performance is measured on a capitalization-weighted basis. The index is maintained by Standard & Poor's Corporation, a subsidiary of The McGraw-Hill Companies.

S&P common stock rankings: The S&P rankings measure historical growth and stability of earnings and dividends. The system includes nine rankings:

A+, A, and A–: Above average

B+: Average

B, B–, and C: Below average

NR: Insufficient historical data or not amenable to the ranking process

As a matter of policy, S&P does not rank the stocks of foreign companies, investment companies, and certain finance-oriented companies.

Securities: A tradable financial instrument.

Securities and Exchange Commission (SEC): The keystone agency in the regulation of securities markets. It governs exchanges, over-the-counter markets, broker-dealers, the conduct of secondary markets, extension of credit in securities transactions, the conduct of corporate insiders, and principally the prohibition of fraud and manipulation in securities transactions.

Securities Investor Protection Corporation (SIPC): A government-sponsored organization created in 1970 to insure investor accounts at brokerage firms in the event of the brokerage firm's insolvency and liquidation. The maximum insurance of $500,000, including a maximum of $100,000 in cash assets per account, covers customer losses due to brokerage house insolvency, not customer losses caused by security price fluctuations. SIPC coverage is conceptually similar to Federal Deposit Insurance Corporation coverage of customer accounts at commercial banks.

Security selection: Process of picking securities, especially stocks for investment purposes.

Shares: Specific portions of tradable equity, a share of stock. It generally refers to common or preferred stocks.

Single premium deferred annuity: An annuity purchased with a lump-sum premium payment which earns interest for a period of years before the payout period begins.

Speculator: A high risk taker. Someone who places large bets for short duration—an hour, a day, a month. He speculates the market or stock will move in the direction of his bet.

Standard deviation: Volatility can be statistically measured using standard deviation. Standard deviation describes how far from the mean historic performance has been, either higher or lower. Mean is simply the middle point between the two historic extremes of the performance of the investment you are examining. The standard deviation measurement helps explain what the distribution of returns likely will be. The greater the range of returns, the greater the risk. Generally, the current price of a security reflects the expected total return of its investment and its perceived risk. The lower the risk, the lower the return expected.

Stock: A contract signifying ownership of a portion of a public or private company.

Stock picker: Someone who is actively trying to select companies whose equity may rise in the short or long term. Valid academic research shows this process is unworkable and results are no better than random.

Strategic asset allocation: Determines an appropriate asset mix for an investor based on long-term capital market conditions, expected returns, and risks.

Subaccount: That portion of the variable annuities separate account that invests in shares of the funds' portfolios. Each subaccount will invest only in a single portfolio.

Systematic withdrawal plan: A program in which shareholders receive payments from their mutual fund investments at regular intervals. Typically, these payments are drawn first from the fund's dividends and capital gains distribution, if any, and then from principal as needed.

Tactical asset allocation: Investment strategy allocating assets according to investor expectations of directions of regional markets and asset classes.

Tax-efficient fund: Money pool that makes no taxable distributions to investors.

Technical analysis: Any investment approach that judges the attractiveness of particular stocks or the market as a whole based on market data, such as price patterns, volume, momentum, or investor sentiment, as opposed to fundamental financial data, such as earnings dividends.

Time horizon: The amount of time someone can wait to generate or take profits from an investment.

Time weighted rate of return: The rate at which a dollar invested at the beginning of a period would grow if no additional capital were invested and no cash withdrawals were made. It provides an indication of value added by the investment manager, and allows comparisons to the performance of other investment managers and market indexes.

Total return: A standard measure of performance or return including both capital appreciation (or depreciation) and dividends or other income received. For example, Stock A is priced at $60 at the start of a year and pays an annual dividend of $4. If the stock moves up to $70 in price, the appreciation component is 16.7 percent, the yield component is 6.7 percent, and the total return is 23.4 percent. That oversimplification does not take into account any earnings on the reinvested dividends.

Trading costs: Fees or commissions paid to move money from one financial instrument to another.

Transaction costs: Another term for execution costs. Any fees or commissions generated and paid in the management of a portfolio. Total transaction costs (or the cost of buying and selling stocks) have three components: (1) the actual dollars paid in commissions, (2) the market impact—that is, the impact a manager's trade has on the market price for the stock (this varies with the size of the trade and the skill of the trader), and (3) the opportunity cost of the return (positive or negative) given up by not executing the trade instantaneously.

Treasury bills: A U.S. financial security issued by Federal Reserve banks for the Treasury as a means of borrowing money for short periods of time. They are sold at a discount from their maturity value, pay no coupons, and have maturities of up to one year. Because they are a direct obligation of the federal government, they are free of default risk. Most Treasury bills are purchased by commercial banks and held as part of their secondary reserves. T-bills regulate the liquidity base of the banking system in order to control the money supply. For example, if the authorities wish to expand the money supply, they can buy Treasury bills, which increase the reserves of the banking system and induce a multiple expansion of bank deposits.

Turnover: Turnover is the volume or percentage of buying or selling activity within a mutual fund portfolio relative to the mutual fund portfolio's size.

12b-1 mutual fund: Mutual fund that assesses shareholders for some of its promotion expenses. These funds are usually no-load, so no brokers are involved in the sale to the public. Instead, the funds normally rely on advertising and public relations to build their assets. The charge usually amounts to about 1 percent or less of a fund's assets. A 12b-1 fund must be specifically registered as such with the Securities and Exchange Commission, and the fact that such charges are levied must be disclosed.

Underperform: Securities or markets that do not meet expectations.

Value added: These are returns over and above those of the stock market.

Value mutual fund: In this instance, the mutual fund manager uses various tests to determine an intrinsic value for a given security, and tries to purchase the security substantially below that value. The goal and hope are that the stock price in the fund will ultimately rise to the stock's fair value or above. Price to earnings, price to sales, price to cash flow, price to book value, and price to break-up value (or true value) are some of the ratios examined in such an approach.

Value stocks: Stocks with high book to market valuations—that is, companies doing poorly in the market that may have the potential to do better.

Variable annuities: Insurance-based investment products, which like other forms of annuities allow for growth of invested premiums to be free from taxation until withdrawals are made from the contract. Unique to variable annuities are several forms of investment alternatives that vary in both potential for reward and risk. Variable annuity choices are broad enough that an investor can employ either an aggressive or conservative approach, or a combination of both, while enjoying the benefits of tax-deferred growth. Guarantee of principal from loss upon death of the owner is covered by a death benefit provision.

Variable annuity accumulation and distribution phases: The two phases of the "life" of an annuity. The initial phase is the accumulation phase. This is the period in which contributions are made, either as a lump-sum or in systematic payments. The contributions are invested in either a fixed or variable annuity. The assets compound tax-deferred until the contract owner makes the decision to distribute (distribution phase) the assets, either in a lump sum or systematically.

Volatility: The extent to which market values and investment returns are uncertain or fluctuate. Another word for risk, volatility is gauged using such measures as beta, mean absolute deviation, and standard deviation.

Weighting: A term usually associated with proportions of assets invested in a particular sector or securities index to generate a specific risk/reward profile.

Yield (current yield): For stocks, yield is the percentage return paid in dividends on a common or preferred stock, calculated by dividing the indicated annual dividend by the market price of the stock. For example, if a stock sells for $40 and pays a dividend of $2 per share, it has a yield of 5 percent (i.e., $2 divided by $40).

For bonds, the coupon rate of interest divided by the market price is called current yield. For example, a bond selling for $1,000 with a 10 percent coupon offers a 10 percent current yield. If the same bond were selling for $500, it would offer a 20 percent yield to an investor who bought it for $500. (As a bond's price falls, its yield rises, and vice versa.)

Yield curve: A chart or graph showing the price of securities (usually fixed income) through time. A flat or inverted yield curve of fixed income instruments is thought by many to be an indicator of recession. This is because those who borrow at the far end of the curve usually pay more for their money than those who borrow for only a little while. When the yield curve is flat or inverted, this means there is little demand for long-term money and this can be interpreted as a signal that there is little demand in the economy for the products that long-term borrowing would generate.

Yield to maturity: The discount rate that equates the present value of the bond's cash flows (semiannual coupon payments and the redemption value) with the market price. The yield to maturity will actually be earned if (1) the investor holds the bond to maturity, and (2) the investor is able to reinvest all coupon payments at a rate equal to the yield to maturity. When a bond is selling at par, the yield to maturity and the coupon rate are equal.

INDEX

Absolute performance, 25
Accounting, mental, 11–12
Accumulation life-cycle phase, 13–14
Accumulation phase (annuities), 95–96, 148
Adjusted gross income (AGI), 22
Adventurer investors, 20, 21, 118
Advisor(s), 117–125, 133
    charges for services by, 124–125
    cost of, 117–118
    and investment personality, 20–23, 118
    obtaining lists of, 124
    qualifications of, 120–121
    reasons for working with, 117
    selecting, 119, 120–124
Aggressive growth, 133
Aggressive portfolio model, 110, 115
AGI (adjusted gross income), 22
Allocation of investments, 17–18
Alternative minimum tax (AMT), 33
American Institute of CPAs, 124
American Stock Exchange, 77, 129
AMT (alternative minimum tax), 33
Analysis, 133
Analysts, 133
Annual interest income, 133
Annuity beneficiary, 133
Annuity(-ies), 90–99, 133
    death benefits from, 97
    deferred, 137
    fixed, 90
    flexible premium, 95, 96
    interest rates for, 97
    investing in, 91–93
    methods of purchase, 94–95
    phases of, 95–97
    single premium, 94–95
    subaccounts, 93–94
    variable, 90, 91–94
Archipelago (TNTO), 130
A-shares, 62
Ask price, 75, 129–130
Asset allocation, 13–16, 42–44, 133, 146
Asset classes, 52–57, 133
    allocation among, 43
    bonds, 52–53
    correlation for, 46, 47

Asset classes (cont.):
    in different markets, 40
    four basic, 52
    international stocks, 54–56
    in mutual funds, 60, 69
    performance of, 40
    spreading risk within, 44
    stocks, 53–56
Asset mix, 134
Asset-class investing, 133
Audits (mutual funds), 67
Average daily trading, 134
Average return, 134
Average(s), 38
    of four model portfolios, 110
    for individual asset classes, 56

Back-end load, 62, 134
Balanced index, 134
Balanced mutual funds, 71, 134
Balanced portfolio model, 110, 113
Bank representatives, 120, 123
Basis point, 134
Bear market, 134
Beginning value, 134
Benchmark, 134
Beta, 24, 38–39, 56, 110, 134–135
Bid prices, 129–130
Bloomberg's Trade Book (BTRD), 131
Blue-chip stocks, 85
Bond funds, 86–87
Bond rating, 135
Bonds, 52–53, 56, 85–89, 135
    buying, 87
    collateralized, 86
    corporate, 87–88
    index for, 70
    information to review before purchasing, 88–89
    listed, 88
    main categories of, 87–88
    mortgage, 86
    municipal, 88
    ratings of, 89
    return/volatility of, 43
    short-term, 55–56

Bonds (cont.):
    trust, 86
    U.S. government, 87
Book value, 71
Book-to-market ratio, 135
Broker-dealer, 135
Broker-directed accounts, 80, 135
Brokers, 102–123
B-shares, 62
BTRD (Bloomberg's Trade Book), 131
Buckets of money, 12, 17–18
Bull markets, 40, 135
Business day, 135
Buy price, 75

Call option, 135
Call risk, 86
Capital appreciation/depreciation, 135
Capital gains/losses, 33, 65, 81
Capital preservation, 136
Cash, 136
Cash equivalents, 43
CDs, 12, 53
Celebrity investors, 20, 21, 118
Certified financial planners (CFPs), 121
Certified investment management consultants (CIMCs), 123
Certified investment management specialists (CIMSs), 123
Certified public accountants (CPAs), 121–122
CFAs (chartered financial analysts), 122
CFPs (certified financial planners), 121
Chartered financial analysts (CFAs), 122
Chartered financial consultants (ChFCs), 121
Chrysler, 78–79
CIMCs (certified investment management consultants), 123
CIMSs (certified investment management specialists), 123
Client-directed fee-based accounts, 80
Clones, 93
Closed-end funds, 77, 78
Collateralized bonds, 86
Commercial paper, 53
Commissions, 62, 124, 125, 136

Commodities, 52
Common stocks, 83–84
Compartmentalization of investments, 11–12
Compound annual return, 136
Compounding, 50–52, 136
Conservative, 136
Conservative portfolio model, 110, 112
Consolidation life-cycle stage, 14, 15
Constraints, 30, 58
Consumer Price Index (CPI), 136
Contrarian investing, 103, 136
Control, sense of, 11
Core savings strategy, 136
Corporate bonds, 85–89
Correction, 136
Correlation, 46–47, 136
Cost(s):
    of advisors, 117–118
    of individually managed accounts, 81
    of mutual funds, 60–63, 81
    transaction, 87, 147
    of variable annuities, 92–93
Coupon, 136
Covariance, 47
CPAs (see Certified public accountants)
CPI (Consumer Price Index), 136
Creation units, 77
Credit cards, borrowing on, 12
Credit risk (U.S. government securities), 87
C-shares, 62
Currency risk, 137
Current return on equity (ROE), 137
Current yield, 137, 149
Custody (mutual funds), 68

Daimler-Benz, 78
Day trading, 131–132
Dealer concessions, 124
Death benefits (annuities), 97
Debentures, 85, 86
Deferred annuity, 137
Deviation, 137
Diamonds, 77
Diet, financial success, 10–11
Discount brokers, 122–123
Dissimilar price movement, 137
Distribution phase (annuities), 148
Diversification, 44–46, 137
    and asset allocation, 43
    effective/ineffective, 45–46
    global, 55, 139
    in mutual funds, 66
Diversified emerging market stocks, 72
Diversified international stocks, 72
Dividend payout ratio, 84–85
Dividend yield, 85
Dividend(s), 65, 83, 137
DJIA (see Dow Jones Industrial Average)
Dollar cost averaging, 51–52, 137
Dow Jones Industrial Average (DJIA), 46, 85, 137
Dow Jones Industrial Average Index, 70

EAFE Index, 55, 56, 70
Earnings per share (EPS) growth, 138
ECNs (see Electronic Communication Networks)
Economies of scale, 61
Efficiency, 138
Efficient frontier, 138
Electronic Communication Networks (ECNs),
    130–131
Emerging growth mutual fund, 138
Emerging market stocks, 54–56, 72
Emerging markets, 138
Emotional curve of investing, 102–103
EPS (earnings per share) growth, 138
Equities, 138
    [See also Stock(s)]
Equity mutual funds, 59, 61, 81
ETFs (see Exchange traded funds)
Everyday money (see Short-term money)
Exchange traded funds (ETFs), 77–79
Execution price, 138
Expected return, 38, 39, 106–107, 138
Expenses, 138

Families, mutual fund, 69, 142
Family plans, 67
Federal tax rates, 32–33
Fee-based, 80, 138
Fee-only, 120, 123, 138
Fees:
    in mutual funds, 61–64
    and portfolio growth, 117
    12b-1, 124
    with variable annuities, 92–93
Financial advisor/planner, 121, 138
    [See also Advisor(s)]
Financial success diet, 10–11
Fixed annuities, 90, 138
Fixed income investments, 53, 55
Fixed income mutual funds, 73–74, 139
Fixed income securities (see Bonds)
Flexible premium annuities, 95, 96
Forecasts, 139
401(k) plans, 99, 139
Front-end load, 62, 139
Full-service brokers, 122
Fund ratings, 139
Fund shares, 139
Fundamentals, 139
Fund(s):
    closed-end, 77, 78
    exchange traded, 77–79
    global bond, 73
    gold, 74
    high-yield fixed income, 73
    index, 61, 70, 76, 126, 139
    international fixed income, 73
    money market, 56, 73–74, 142
    municipal bond, 73
    mutual [see Mutual fund(s)]
    real estate, 74
    sector, 74

Fund(s) (cont.):
    tax-efficient, 146
    technology, 74
    U.S. fixed income, 73
    utilities, 74

Gifting life-cycle stage, 16
Global bond funds, 73
Global diversification, 55, 139
Gold funds, 74
Government bonds, 53, 56
Government fixed income funds, 73
Growth:
    aggressive, 133
    compounding for, 51
    earnings per share, 138
    as return, 39
    and risk, 53
    and volatility of investments, 24
Growth companies, 54, 55
Growth portfolio model, 110, 114
Growth stocks, 71
Guardian investors, 20, 22, 118
Guided managed account programs, 80

High-yield fixed income funds, 73
High-yield bonds, 53
Hot stocks, 41–42
Hot tip, 139
HR-10 plans, 99

Icons, 4
IIMC (Institute for Investment Management
    Consultants), 123
INCA (see InstiNet)
Income, adjusted gross/taxable, 33
Income growth mutual funds, 139
Index funds, 61, 70, 76, 126, 139
Indexes, 70
Indexing, 140
Individual investor, 140
Individual retirement accounts (IRAs), 99–100
Individualist investors, 20, 22, 118
Individually managed accounts, 80–82
Inflation, 140
Inherited wealth, 22, 23
Initial public offerings (IPOs), 83, 140
InstiNet (INCA), 130, 131
Institute for Investment Management Consultants
    (IIMC), 123
Institute of Certified Financial Planners, 124
Institutional investors, 87, 140
Interest, 140
Interest rates, 86, 97
Interest-rate risk, 86
International equities, 72
International fixed income funds, 73
International growth stocks, 72
International stocks, 54–56, 70, 72

International value stocks, 72
Intrinsic value, 140
Invest, 140
Investing:
    for $1 million by age 65, 14
    comparison to dieting, 10–11
    contrarian, 103, 136
    day trading vs., 131
    emotional curve of, 102–103
    long-term, 47–50
    momentum, 103
    online, 130–132
    process of, 10–11
    rules of, 37–41
    (*See also specific topics*)
Investment advisors, 68
    [*See also* Advisor(s)]
Investment Company Act of 1950, 68
Investment Company Institute, 63
Investment discipline, 140
Investment management consultants, 123
Investment objective, 63, 140
Investment philosophy, 140
Investment policy statement (IPS), 2, 7–9, 105,
    107, 116, 125, 140
Investment pools (*see* Buckets of money)
Investment strategies, 41–57, 100
    adding time to, 47–50
    asset allocation, 42–44
    asset-class investing, 52–57
    combining dissimilar investments, 46–47
    compounding, 50–52
    diversification, 44–46
    (*See also specific topics*)
Investment vehicles, 57–100
    annuities, 90–99
    bonds, 85–89
    exchange traded funds, 77–79
    individually managed accounts, 80–82
    mutual funds [*see* Mutual fund(s)]
    retirement plans, 98–100
    stocks, 82–85
Investment wisdom, 140
Investor discomfort, 140
Investor personalities, 19–23, 118
IPOs (*see* Initial public offerings)
IPS (*see* Investment policy statement)
IRAs (*see* Individual retirement accounts)
Island (ISLD), 131
Issue specific risk, 101

Keogh plans, 99

Large-cap growth mutual funds, 70
Large-cap growth stocks, 71
Large-cap stocks, 54, 56
Large-cap value mutual funds, 70
Large-cap value stocks, 71
Legal considerations, 34

Licensed Independent Network of CPA Financial
    Planners (LINC), 124
Life stages, 12–16
Lifeboat drill, 25–29
Limited partnerships, 69
LINC (Licensed Independent Network of CPA
    Financial Planners), 124
Lipper Analytical Services, 76
Liquidity, 31, 66, 140
Listed bonds, 88
Listed exchanges, 129
Listed stocks, 128
Load funds, 62, 140
Long-term bonds, 56
Long-term investing, 47–50
Long-term money, 12, 17, 18
    and equity mutual funds, 59
    and investing for $1 million by age 65, 14
    IPS section for, 8–9
    legal considerations/unique circumstances
        related to, 35
    lifeboat drill, 28
    target growth rate for, 106–107
    time horizon for, 30
Long-term thinking, 38
Lump-sum distribution, 141

Major purchase money (*see* Mid-term money)
Management fees, 61, 141
Management of mutual funds, 64, 69
Margin, 141
Market bottom, 141
Market capitalization, 141
Market rates, 86
Market risk, 24, 101
Market timing, 42, 101–102, 141
Market value, 141
Market(s), 141
    bear, 134
    bull, 40
    fluctuations in, 47
    over-the-counter (OTC), 129–130, 143
    top performing, 40
Maturity (bonds), 53, 85–89, 141
Mean, 38
Mental accounting, 11–12
Mid-cap growth stocks, 71
Mid-cap value stocks, 71
Mid-term money, 12, 17, 18
    and equity mutual funds, 59
    IPS section for, 8
    lifeboat drill, 27
    target growth rate for, 106–107
    time horizon for, 30
Minimums, in mutual funds, 63
Mistakes of first time investors, 24–25
Model portfolio(s), 110–116, 142
Modern portfolio theory, 142
Momentum investing, 103

Money:
    categories of, 12
    retirement, 8–9, 12, 18
    serious, 1
    (*See also* Long-term money; Mid-term money;
        Short-term money)
Money managers, 125
Money market funds, 56, 73–74, 142
Moody's bond rating services, 89
Morgan Stanley, 70
Mortgage bonds, 86
Municipal bond funds, 73
Municipal bonds, 88, 142
Mutual fund managed accounts, 80
Mutual fund wraps, 80
Mutual fund(s), 58–77, 142
    advantages of ETFs over, 78
    asset-class subcategories of, 69
    audited performance of, 67
    balanced, 71
    bonds in, 87
    choosing, 59
    costs in, 60–63
    diversification in, 44, 66
    dividends from, 65
    emerging growth, 138
    families of, 69, 142
    fixed income, 73–74
    income growth, 139
    and individually managed accounts, 80–82
    initial investment in, 66
    liquidity provided by, 66
    loaded, 62
    management fees in, 61
    municipal bonds in, 88
    professional managers of, 66
    prospectuses for, 63–65
    quality growth, 143–144
    reading newspaper tables of, 75–76
    reinvestment in, 67
    relationship of various parties to, 68–69
    sales charges in, 62
    small caps, 70
    statements from, 65
    stock funds, 71–72
    switching in, 67
    taxes in, 58
    top 1999 performers, 59
    turnover in, 67
    12b-1, 124, 148
    underperforming, 76–77
    U.S. equities, 70
    value mutual, 148
    and variable annuity subaccount investment, 93
    working of, 60–63

NASDAQ Composite, 48–49, 70, 130, 131
National Association of Securities Dealers, Inc.
    (NASD), 120, 142
NAV (*see* Net asset value)

NAV price per share, 75, 76
Net asset value (NAV), 60, 66, 142
Net gain/losses, 66
Net trade, 142
New York Stock Exchange (NYSE), 128, 129
Newspaper mutual fund tables, 75–76
No-load funds, 62–63, 142–143
No-load variable annuities, 92
Nominal return, 143
NYSE (*see* New York Stock Exchange)

Offer (ask price), 75, 129
Online stock investing, 130–132
Open auction market, 129
Operating expenses, 143
Optimization, 143
OTC Bulletin Board, 129
OTC market (*see* Over-the-counter market)
Outperform, 143
Over-the-counter (OTC) market, 129–130, 143
Owners, lenders vs., 37–38

Payout phase (annuities), 96–97
Perceived risk, 38–39
Percentage points, 143
Performance:
    absolute, 25
    and asset allocation, 43–44
    diversification and, 44
    mutual fund/individually managed account
        reporting of, 82
    of mutual funds, 59–60, 63
    relative, as risk measure, 24–25
    time horizon for measurement of, 48
    top market, 40
Perot, Ross, 88
Personal financial specialists (PFSs), 121–122
Personalities, investor (*see* Investor personalities)
Personally advised accounts, 80
PFSs (*see* Personal financial specialists)
Portfolio management, 126–132
Portfolio turnover, 143
Portfolios, 42
    and asset allocation, 43, 44
    consistency in, 46
    customization of, 81
    model, 110–116, 142
    overall risk of, 46, 55–56
    of volatile stocks, 47
Preferred stock, 84
Price/earnings (P/E) ratios, 71, 84, 143
Price(s):
    ask, 75, 129–130
    bid, 129–130
    of bonds, 86–87
    buy, 75
    execution, 138
    offer, 75
Principal, 143
Prospectus, 63, 143

Public utilities, 85–86
Put, 143

Quality growth mutual funds, 143–144
Quartile, 144

Rate of return, 106–108, 144
    on fixed annuities, 90
    of four model portfolios, 110
    for individual asset classes, 56
    risk and, 110
    time weighted, 147
    on variable annuities, 92
Ratings, 144
    bonds, 89
    mutual fund, 76
Real estate funds, 74
Real estate investment, 38–39, 52
Real estate investment trusts (REITs), 144
Real return, 144
Rebalancing, 144
RediBook (REDI), 131
Registered investment advisors (RIAs), 122
Reinvested dividends, 144
Reinvesting, 50, 67
REITs (real estate investment trusts), 144
Relative performance, 24–25
Relative return, 144
Relative risk, 38
Retirement money, 12, 18
    (*See also* Long-term money)
Retirement plans, 98–100
Return on investment (ROI), 145
Return(s), 106–107
    annualized after-tax, 108
    compound annual, 136
    for different investment classes, 40
    expected (*see* Expected return)
    growth as, 39
    and level of decline, 106–107
    in mutual funds, 59, 60
    real, 144
    since WWII, 41
    stability vs., 55
    total, 43
    variation in, 43–44
RIAs (registered investment advisors), 122
Risk, 144
    call, 86
    currency, 137
    diminishing, over time, 47–50
    and expected return, 38
    and growth, 53
    interest-rate, 86
    of investing directly in bonds, 86–89
    issue specific, 101
    levels of, 38–39
    of major bond types, 87–88
    market, 24, 101
    and maturity, 53

Risk (*cont.*):
    in mutual funds, 64
    perceived, 38–39
    and rate of return, 110
    in real estate vs. other investments, 38–39
    relative vs. total, 38
    and size of company, 53
    spreading, within an asset class, 44
    standard measurements of, 38–39
    systematic vs. unsystematic, 101
    and volatility, 39
Risk management, 70
Risk measurement, 24–26, 38
Risk tolerance, 145
Risk-free rate of return, 144
Riskometer scale, 57, 71–73, 106
Risky investments, 39
ROE (current return on equity), 137
ROI (return on investment), 145
Roth IRAs, 100
Rules of investing, 37–41
Russell 1000 Indexes, 70
Russell 2000 Indexes, 70

Sales charges, in mutual funds, 62
Savings Incentive Match Plan for Employees
    (SIMPLE), 99
Screen based market, 130
SEC (*see* Securities and Exchange Commission)
Sector funds, 74
Securities, 145
Securities and Exchange Commission (SEC),
    64–65, 67, 131, 145
Securities Investor Protection Corporation
    (SIPC), 145
Security selection, 145
Separately managed accounts (*see* Individually
    managed accounts)
SEP-IRAs, 98
SEPs (simplified employee pensions), 98
Serious money, 1
Services (mutual fund), 64
Share price, of mutual funds, 58
Shares, 64, 145
Shearson Lehman Aggregate Bond Index, 70
Short-term bonds, 55–56
Short-term money, 12, 17, 18
    and equity mutual funds, 59
    IPS section for, 7–8
    lifeboat drill, 26
    target growth rate for, 106–107
    time horizon for, 30
SIMPLE (Savings Incentive Match Plan for
    Employees), 99
Simplified employee pensions (SEPs), 98
Single premium annuities, 94–95
Single premium deferred annuity, 146
SIPC (Securities Investor Protection
    Corporation), 145
Size of companies, 53
Small Cap, 129

Small caps mutual funds, 70
Small-cap growth stocks, 71
Small-cap stocks, 54, 56
Small-cap value stocks, 71
S&P 500 (*see* Standard & Poor's 500)
Specialists (stock exchange), 129
Specialty funds, 74
Specific risk, 101
Speculations, 48
Speculator, 146
Spending life-cycle stage, 15–16
Spiders, 77
Spread, 130
Standard & Poor's 500 (S&P 500), 46, 55, 70,
    85, 110, 116, 145
Standard & Poor's bond rating services, 89
Standard & Poor's common stock ratings, 145
Standard deviation, 38, 146
    (*See also* Volatility)
State tax rates, 32, 33
Stock exchanges, 83, 127–129
Stock funds, 71–72
Stock market(s), 40–41, 55, 129
Stock mutual funds, 44, 59
Stock picker, 146
Stock portfolios, 47
Stockbrokers, 120
Stock(s), 53–56, 82–85, 146
    blue-chip, 85
    common, 83–84
    constraints for, 58
    dividend payout ratio, 84–85
    dividend yield, 85
    investment vehicles for, 58
    listed, 128
    and market timing, 101–102
    online investing in, 130–132
    picking individual, 101
    preferred, 84
    price/earnings ratio of, 84
    prices of, 83
    return/volatility of, 43
    short-term holdings in, 48

Stock(s) (*cont.*):
    trading, on the exchanges, 128–129
    volatility of, 39
Straight-arrow investors, 20, 22
Strategic asset allocation, 146
Strategies, investment (*see* Investment strategies)
Subaccounts (variable annuities), 93–94, 146
Switching, 67
Systematic withdrawal plan, 146

Tactical asset allocation, 146
Target growth rate, 106–107
Tax rates, 32–33
Taxable income, 33
Tax-efficient fund, 146
Taxes:
    alternative minimum, 33
    on bonds, 88
    control of, 109
    on ETFs, 78
    impact of, 108–109
    on individually managed accounts, 81
    and investment vehicles, 58, 88, 90
    on mutual funds earnings, 65
    and retirement plans, 98–100
    and switching of mutual funds, 67
    on variable annuities, 92
Technical analysis, 146–147
Technology funds, 74
Time horizon, 30, 147
    for long-term money, 13
    for performance measurement, 48
    to retirement, 14, 15
    in spending life-cycle stage, 15
    for stocks, 56
Time weighted rate of return, 147
Timing, market (*see* Market timing)
TNTO (Archipelago), 130
Total return, 43–44, 147
Total risk, 38
Trade-offs, 37
Trading costs, 147

Trading Floor (NYSE), 128
Traditional IRAs, 99–100
Transaction costs, 87, 147
Treasury bills, 53, 147
Treasury bonds, 53
Triple A rated bonds, 53
Trust bonds, 86
Turnover, 67, 143, 147
12b-1 mutual funds, 124, 148

Umbrella plans, 67
Underperform, 148
Unique circumstances, 35
Unsystematic risk, 101
U.S. fixed income funds, 73
U.S. government notes/bonds, 87
U.S. stocks, 54, 55
Utilities, 85–86
Utilities funds, 74

Value added, 148
Value companies, 54, 55
Value mutual fund, 148
Value stocks, 71, 148
Vanguard Indexes, 76
Vanguard S&P 500 fund, 70
Variable annuities, 58, 65, 90–94, 148
Vehicles, investment (*see* Investment vehicles)
Volatility, 24, 38, 39, 43, 148

Weighting, 149
Withdrawals from annuities, 90, 92

Yield curve, 149
Yield(s), 149
    of bonds, 86
    of corporate bonds, 87–88
    dividend, 85
    to maturity, 149

ABOUT THE AUTHORS

Joe John Duran, CFA, is president of Centurion Capital Management and a member of the Board of Directors for Centurion Capital Group, Inc.

Centurion is a nationally registered investment company with over $2 billion in client assets, over 12,000 client accounts, and a team of CFAs, Ph.D.s, and MBAs dedicated to one mission—managing investors' serious money.

Joe joined the firm in 1992 and was instrumental in growing CCM from $100 million in assets under management to $2 billion over an eight-year span. In that time, he helped to develop many industry-pioneering investment strategies and services primarily targeted toward helping individual investors access the tools typically reserved for institutions.

Joe has appeared nationally in print and broadcast media discussing investing for individuals and institutions. As a speaker at investing symposiums and workshops nationally, he has helped thousands of investors and their advisors. His focus has been in helping investors understand the complexities of investing, and to help their advisors to build successful practices.

Joe holds the Chartered Financial Analyst designation and is a fellow of the Association of Investment Management and Research, a member of the Los Angeles Society of Financial Analysts, and a member of the Association of Investment Management Sales Executives. Joe graduated with a joint degree in Finance and Marketing from Saint Louis University. Besides the CFA, Joe holds the series 2, 63, and 65 licenses.

Larry Chambers is a freelance writer, coach-writer, and author based in Ojai, CA. He has built a reputation in the financial securities industry helping the already successful achieve their *next* level by writing and placing client articles and books in national trade magazines and with major publishing houses including McGraw-Hill, Random House, Times Mirror, Dow Jones, Irwin, and John Wiley and Sons. He has authored over 30 books and 700 investment related articles.

Chambers' background is with a major Wall Street wirehouse. He joined EF Hutton & Co. as a stockbroker, where he achieved an outstanding track record, becoming an associate vice president and was named one of the top 20 brokers out of more than 5,000. He received numerous awards and was a member of the Blue Chip Club.